THE
TACO
TUESDAY
COOKBOOK

THE
TACO
TUESDAY
COOKBOOK

52 TASTY TACO RECIPES TO
MAKE EVERY WEEK THE BEST EVER

Laura Fuentes
Founder of MOMables.com

FAIR WINDS

Inspiring | Educating | Creating | Entertaining

Brimming with creative inspiration, how-to projects, and useful information to enrich your everyday life, Quarto Knows is a favorite destination for those pursuing their interests and passions. Visit our site and dig deeper with our books into your area of interest: Quarto Creates, Quarto Cooks, Quarto Homes, Quarto Lives, Quarto Drives, Quarto Explores, Quarto Gifts, or Quarto Kids.

First Published in 2018 by Fair Winds Press, an imprint of The Quarto Group,
100 Cummings Center, Suite 265-D, Beverly, MA 01915, USA.
T (978) 282-9590 F (978) 283-2742 QuartoKnows.com

Fair Winds Press titles are also available at discount for retail, wholesale, promotional, and bulk purchase. For details, contact the Special Sales Manager by email at specialsales@quarto.com or by mail at The Quarto Group, Attn: Special Sales Manager, 100 Cummings Center, Suite 265-D, Beverly, MA 01915, USA.

22 21   11

ISBN: 978-1-59233-819-1

Digital edition published in 2018

Library of Congress Cataloging-in-Publication Data

Fuentes, Laura (Chef), author.
The taco Tuesday cookbook : 52 tasty taco recipes to make every week
   the best ever / Laura Fuentes.
ISBN 9781592338191 (pbk.)
1. Tacos. 2. Mexican American cooking. 3. Cookbooks.
TX836 .F84 2018
641.84--dc23
LCCN 2018012263

Design: Rita Sowins / Sowins Design
Cover Image: Alison Bickel Photography
Page Layout: Rita Sowins/Sowins Design
Photography: Alison Bickel Photography

Printed in China

TO ALL THE TACO LOVERS OUT THERE:
MAY THE RECIPES IN THIS BOOK
GIVE YOU SOMETHING TO TACOBOUT

CONTENTS

MÁS! REFRESHING BEVERAGES ... 147

INTRODUCTION

It might seem obvious that I love tacos. I mean, who sets out to eat tacos once a week for a year and then write a book about it?

That would be me. I spent almost two years eating tacos weekly, if not two or three times per week. Whenever I went out to eat, I'd always order tacos and then make notes on my phone about what was in the taco so I could remember when recreating it at home. And my camera roll on my phone? I am afraid to tell you how many taco photos are in there.

I'm crazy for tacos. I like tacos for breakfast, lunch, and dinner. There's something about having a vessel like a tortilla to hold together all of the decadent flavors of a taco filling—and of course the accompaniments and the sauces drizzled on top. It's the whole package.

Unlike most Americans, however, I didn't grow up eating tacos. I'm from Spain, so I had never even heard of a taco until I moved to the United States in my teens. I remember my first taco experience quite clearly. It was taco day at my high school cafeteria in California. That day I had forgotten my lunch, something my mom so neatly packed every day. So, I went to the cafeteria and saw tacos on the menu.

If you're not familiar with cafeteria tacos, they are nothing to write home about. What I found that day was barely seasoned, greasy ground meat in a soggy tortilla, topped with wilted lettuce and shredded cheese. Yes, it was as bad as it sounds. I couldn't understand what the big deal about taco day was all about, and this experience solidified that idea.

It's also important to note that I did not grow up eating Mexican food or spicy food. So whenever I went out to eat with my mom or friends, Mexican food was never on the horizon for me. When I did go, the only thing I would order was plain chicken nachos: chips + cheese + grilled chicken. The end.

How exactly does one become taco-obsessed after the worst taco experience ever?

Allow me to tell you about my first real taco experience. From that day on, my love for Mexican food was born.

I was thirteen years old. I went to Sea World with my mom, my first American friend, Ashley, and her dad. After a long day seeing the sights, we were all starving. We were unfamiliar with the area, and after leaving the park my mom said that it would have to be Mexican food or Mexican food because there was nothing else around. "But Mom, I don't like Mexican food!" I remember telling her. She calmly replied that it was either Mexican tonight or waiting until food the next day. So Mexican food it was.

I ordered the mixed taco platter because I didn't know what else to do. I was convinced that the food would be very spicy and that I wouldn't like it. And I was set to prove to my mom that all the things I always thought about tacos were true: they were simply not for me.

When the large platter of tacos arrived at the table, I looked at the variety of fresh ingredients stuffed inside crispy corn and soft tortillas. They were nothing like the cafeteria tacos I was so disappointed with a few months earlier. These tacos were well seasoned, with a smoky flavor I now appreciate from my Arriba! Seasoning (page 88). I started with the flaky grilled fish taco, and with each bite, I savored the freshness of the seafood. I moved on to the shrimp tacos, which were perfectly grilled and blackened. My mouth watered with the short ribs beef taco, not to be undermined by the perfectly juicy chicken taco. Before I realized it, I was hooked.

Years later, I still order tacos on the menu every time I go to a Mexican restaurant. They are my gauge to see if the restaurant's food is average or if there something special about the seasoning, the condiments, and all the other fresh ingredients that can easily be packed and stuffed inside a crispy taco shell or soft tortilla.

When it comes to tacos, I prefer a crispy taco shell even if the eating is messier and I can't stuff as much inside. My family, however, prefers the softer texture that only a flour tortilla can provide, so having both on hand is always a good idea.

In this book, you'll notice a mix of corn, flour, and crunchy tacos throughout. It's up to you how you choose to enjoy your tacos.

When the idea for this cookbook was born, I already had dozens of taco recipes on my websites, LauraFuentes.com and MOMables.com. The hardest part of putting together this book was narrowing it down to 52 main taco recipes (one for each week of the year) that were never published before. I probably could have made it every day instead! Maybe that will be the sequel.

I sincerely hope you take on the weekly tradition of Taco Tuesdays in your home and share your creations from this book with the #TacoTuesdayBook hashtag on Instagram.

TACO TUESDAY: A WEEKLY PARTY

Few things are more exciting to eat than a delicious fresh, homemade taco. When your taste buds meet the contents of a generously stuffed tortilla, that's when the party really gets started. I should know, since I've eaten my share of tacos—and I keep wanting more.

In this cookbook, you'll find everything you need to make Taco Tuesday the best night of the week. Each recipe has been carefully crafted to create a satisfying meal for you, your family, and friends. Because really, tacos are best consumed with loved ones.

The tacos are organized by type of filling—breakfast inspired, vegetarian, chicken, beef, pork, and seafood. I believe this is the best assortment of tacos out there, all at your fingertips. Whenever possible, I've made sure to include helpful tips in the recipes to make prep and cooking a breeze, so even if your weeknights are a little hectic, you can make taco night possible!

You'll also find some of the recipes featured in this book on my MOMables YouTube channel. With this book and the videos, taco night is sure to become your most requested night of the week!

SWITCH UP YOUR TACOS!

There's much more to tacos than the filling. In this book, you'll find a wide variety of tacos that came together by the simple act of playing around with the ingredients and reinventing them in tasty ways.

Breakfast tacos made with eggs, vegetarian tacos featuring my favorite veggies, chicken tacos, beef tacos, pork tacos, and seafood tacos . . . regardless of which taco filling you choose, there's a variety of ingredients to make everyone happy.

Add or swap out some of the toppings or sauces, and you can reinvent any of the 52 recipes into a brand-new taco. The sauces also make terrific salad dressings—all you have to do is add a little water to thin it out!

The recipes in this book can be mixed and matched with the taco builders as well. In the end, my go-to taco builder is always either a crunchy corn tortilla or a grain-free tortilla. On occasion, I throw everything on top of a tostada and enjoy a messy meal.

The Arriba! Seasoning has made three appearances in my cookbooks; it's that good! It's my go-to, all-purpose, make-everything-awesome seasoning, and I'm sure it will soon become yours, too.

TACO BASICS

The only "rule" for making perfect tacos is to read the recipe from start to finish first and then get to it. Using fresh ingredients helps, too. And remember that you can swap items like shrimp for chicken or black beans in your favorite recipes and still have an awesome taco dinner.

TACOS

You'll notice that nearly all the taco recipes in this book have been photographed inside a tortilla. Whether it's in a crunchy or soft tortilla, on a tostada, or in a lettuce cup to keep things lighter, they are all considered "tacos" in my book.

TACO BOWLS

All of these taco recipes can also be served over rice, creating the perfect taco bowl. This allows you to stretch your food budget while also increasing the yield of each recipe. My family also loves the DIY factor that taco bowls provide.

SALADS

Of course, it goes without saying that any leftover taco filling can be used to top a bed of field greens or romaine lettuce. For this very reason, I chose not to include any salad recipes in this book, allowing you to make the most out of every recipe here.

CHAPTER 1

THE ESSENTIALS

Without these, you'd have just the filling—
and that's just *no bueno*.

CLASSIC GUACAMOLE

YIELD: 4 TO 6 SERVINGS

I love serving guacamole at parties because it's always a hit with my guests. This is the perfect recipe to make for a crowd or taco night for the family.

3 avocados, halved and pitted
1 medium shallot, chopped
1 Roma tomato, seeds and pulp removed, diced
3 tablespoons (3 g) finely chopped fresh cilantro
2 garlic cloves, minced
½ medium jalapeño, seeded and diced
½ lime, juiced
½ teaspoon salt

Scoop the flesh of the avocados into a large bowl and use a fork to roughly mash it, making sure you leave a few chunks behind.

Add the remaining ingredients and mix well to combine. Cover and refrigerate until ready to serve. Prior to serving, mix the guacamole around to freshen up the color.

EASY GUACAMOLE

YIELD: 4 TO 6 SERVINGS

Don't have everything you need to make Homemade Guacamole? No problem! This recipe comes together in seconds— no chopping required.

3 ripe avocados, halved and pitted
½ cup (130 g) Pico de Gallo (page 23) or store-bought fresh salsa

Scoop the flesh of the avocados into a large bowl and use a fork to roughly mash it, making sure you leave a few chunks behind.

Mix in the pico de gallo and serve. Cover and refrigerate leftovers. Prior to serving, mix the guacamole around to freshen up the color.

RESTAURANT-STYLE SALSA

YIELD: 12 SERVINGS, ABOUT 4 CUPS (950 ML)

This salsa requires minimal effort, contains zero additives, and results in 100 percent satisfaction every time. Bring on the chips!

1 can (15-ounce/428 g) diced fire-roasted tomatoes, with liquid
1 can (15-ounce/428 g) petite diced tomatoes, with liquid
1 small onion, roughly chopped
1 or 2 jalapeños, seeded
3 garlic cloves, peeled
1½ teaspoons ground cumin
1 teaspoon salt
1 lime, juiced
⅓ cup (5 g) chopped fresh cilantro

Add all the ingredients in the order listed to your blender or food processor. Pulse to combine, then blend on medium speed, gradually increasing to high speed until the texture is nearly smooth.

Transfer to a bowl, cover, and refrigerate for 1 hour prior to serving. Store leftovers in an airtight container in the refrigerator for up to a week.

‹ PINEAPPLE SALSA

....

YIELD: 12 SERVINGS, ABOUT 4 CUPS (950 G)

One day, wanting to add a little oomph to my classic Pico de Gallo (see recipe at right), I added half of a fresh pineapple I had in the fridge. Not only did it transform the fresh salsa into something sweet, but the jalapeño's heat really balanced it out.

2 cups (310 g) diced pineapple
5 Roma tomatoes, seeded and finely diced
½ large red onion, finely diced
½ jalapeño, seeded and finely chopped
½ cup (8 g) chopped fresh cilantro (stems and leaves)
3 garlic cloves, minced
½ lime, juiced
½ teaspoon salt

In a large bowl, combine the pineapple, tomatoes, onion, jalapeño, cilantro, and garlic. Add the lime juice and salt and stir to combine. Serve right away or refrigerate until ready to use.

Store leftovers in an airtight container in the refrigerator for up to 5 days.

||||||||||||||||||||||||||||||||||||||||||||||||

LAURA'S TIP: Switch up this recipe from time to time by swapping out the pineapple for diced mango or peach.

PICO DE GALLO

....

YIELD: 6 SERVINGS

This homemade chunky fresh salsa is the perfect companion to any taco. Or salad, or fried eggs, or seafood ... okay, it's perfect on almost everything!

5 Roma tomatoes, seeded and finely diced
½ large red onion, finely diced
½ jalapeño, seeded and finely chopped
½ cup (8 g) chopped fresh cilantro (stems and leaves)
3 garlic cloves, minced
½ lime, juiced
½ teaspoon salt

In a large bowl, combine the tomatoes, onion, jalapeño, cilantro, and garlic. Add the lime juice and salt and stir to combine. Serve right away or refrigerate until ready to use.

Store leftovers in an airtight container in the refrigerator for up to 5 days.

SALSA VERDE

YIELD: 8 SERVINGS

Roasted tomatillo salsa is sweet, a bit tangy, and absolutely delicious. You'll find tomatillos near the tomatoes in your grocery store; they look like green vine tomatoes in a brown husk.

3 pounds (1.5 kg) tomatillos, husked and halved
1 pint (285 g) cherry tomatoes
1 large jalapeño, halved and seeded
2 shallots, halved
6 to 8 garlic cloves, peeled
1 bunch cilantro, chopped (stems and leaves)
1 lime, juiced
½ teaspoon salt

Place a rack in the middle of the oven and pre-heat the oven's broiler on high.

Spread out the tomatillos, cherry tomatoes, jalapeño, shallots, and garlic cloves in a large roasting pan. Roast for 5 minutes, or until toma-tillos and shallots start to blacken. Flip vegeta-bles over and roast for 5 minutes more, or until the vegetables soften and are slightly charred.

Remove the pan from the oven and allow the vegetables to cool for about 15 minutes.

Transfer the roasted vegetables to a food processor or blender and add the cilantro, lime, and salt. Pulse until the salsa verde is smooth. Allow salsa to cool, then refrigerate in an airtight container for up to 1 week. Enjoy at room temperature or cold.

EASY PICKLED › JALAPEÑOS AND ONIONS

YIELD: 6 TO 8 SERVINGS

For a little added spice on demand, these pickled jalapeños and onions are just the per-fect topper to any taco or salad, or even over scrambled eggs. Make them milder by removing the jalapeño seeds prior to pickling.

1 cup (235 ml) distilled white vinegar
1 cup (235 ml) water
2 tablespoons (13 g) sugar
1 teaspoon whole black peppercorns
½ teaspoon kosher salt
4 large jalapeños, seeded if desired and sliced into rounds
1 medium red onion, sliced
3 or 4 cilantro sprigs, chopped

In a small saucepan, combine the vinegar, water, sugar, peppercorns, and kosher salt. Add the jalapeños and sliced onion and bring to a boil over medium heat. Remove the pan from the heat and transfer the mixture to a jar. Add the chopped cilantro, allow it to cool down to room temperature, and cover. Store in the refrigerator for up to 2 weeks. Enjoy chilled.

CILANTRO CHIMICHURRI

YIELD: ABOUT 1½ CUPS (375 G)

Looking for a new BFF? This cilantro chimichurri is a great complement to any taco, or over steak or fried eggs. You'll find you want to use it on everything!

½ jalapeño, seeded if desired
2 garlic cloves, peeled
¼ cup (40 g) chopped onion
1 packed cup (20 g) fresh cilantro (about 1 bunch), stems and leaves
1 packed cup (20 g) fresh flat-leaf parsley (about 1 bunch), stems and leaves
½ cup (120 ml) extra virgin olive oil
¼ cup (60 ml) lime juice (about 2 limes)
2 teaspoons ground cumin
¾ teaspoon kosher salt

In a food processor, pulse the jalapeño, garlic, and onion several times, until chopped. Add the cilantro and parsley and pulse again. Add the oil, lime juice, cumin, and salt. Pulse until combined.

Use immediately or transfer to an airtight container and refrigerate for up to 1 week.

CILANTRO-LIME DRESSING

YIELD: ABOUT 1 CUP (230 G)

This is my ultimate dressing for tacos. It's super creamy and flavorful, and it complements my tacos and salads perfectly!

½ cup (115 g) sour cream
¼ cup (60 ml) milk
½ lime, juiced
1 teaspoon garlic powder
Pinch salt
Pinch freshly ground black pepper
2 tablespoons (2 g) finely chopped fresh cilantro

In a blender, blend the sour cream, milk, lime, garlic powder, salt, and pepper. Once combined, add the cilantro and pulse to combine.

Use immediately or transfer to an airtight container and refrigerate for up to 5 days.

LAURA'S TIP: You can replace the sour cream with mayonnaise if desired.

EL GRIEGO SAUCE ›

YIELD: ABOUT 1½ CUPS (345 G)

My dad drizzles this sauce over everything, and when he adds it to his tacos, they become Griego (Greek) tacos. It's also great on sandwiches, as a salad dressing, and over roasted veggies.

1 medium cucumber, peeled
1 garlic clove, peeled
1 cup (230 g) plain yogurt
2 teaspoons fresh lemon juice
½ teaspoon salt
¼ teaspoon dried dill

Grate the cucumber and garlic clove into a bowl. Add the yogurt, lemon juice, salt, and dill and mix well. Cover and refrigerate for at least 1 hour prior to serving.

Store leftovers in an airtight container in the refrigerator for up to 5 days.

‹ SRIRACHA-LIME DRESSING

YIELD: 4 TO 6 SERVINGS, ABOUT ½ CUP (118 ML)

This explosive flavor combination will upgrade any cooked meat, not just tacos.

⅓ cup (80 g) sour cream
¼ cup (60 g) cup mayonnaise
1 lime, juiced
1 teaspoon Sriracha sauce, more to taste
1 teaspoon garlic powder

In a medium bowl, combine the sour cream, mayonnaise, lime juice, Sriracha, and garlic powder and mix well. Taste and add more Sriracha as desired.

Use immediately or transfer to an airtight container and refrigerate for up to 5 days.

LAURA'S TIP: If you prefer a thinner consistency, add 1 to 2 tablespoons (15 to 30 ml) water.

THAI PEANUT SAUCE

YIELD: ABOUT ½ CUP (118 ML)

Ridiculously good on salads, as a dip for grilled meats, and, of course, over tacos!

⅓ cup (85 g) creamy peanut butter
2 tablespoons (40 g) honey
1 tablespoon (15 ml) lime juice (about ½ lime)
1 tablespoon (15 ml) soy sauce
1 teaspoon Sriracha sauce
1 garlic clove, grated
2 teaspoons (10 g) grated fresh ginger
1 to 2 tablespoons (15 to 30 ml) hot water

In a small bowl, whisk together the peanut butter, honey, lime juice, soy sauce, Sriracha, garlic, and ginger. Add 1 tablespoon (15 ml) water and whisk to combine. For a thinner sauce, add up to 1 additional tablespoon (15 ml) water to achieve the consistency you'd like.

CORN TORTILLAS

YIELD: 12 TORTILLAS

Tacos aren't complete without corn tortillas, right? This classic three-ingredient recipe can be made in a single bowl. Refrigerate any extra dough balls (wrapped in plastic) for up to 3 days. It's one recipe that never disappoints.

2 cups (252 g) fine corn flour (masa harina)
½ teaspoon sea salt
1½ cups (353 ml) hot water

In a large bowl, whisk together the masa harina and salt.

Pour the hot water into the bowl and mix the dough with a wooden spoon or your hands (be very careful) to form a big ball. The dough should be firm and springy when touched, not dry or super sticky. If the mixture is too dry, add more water by the tablespoon (15 ml) until the dough is the right consistency. It should feel similar to kids' playdough.

Cover the bowl with a tea towel or plastic wrap and allow the dough to rest for about an hour.

Use your hands to form 12 equal-size dough balls. Place a dough ball between two pieces of parchment paper. If you are using a tortilla press, simply press down to flatten. If you are using a rolling pin, roll the dough into a thin, 6-inch (15 cm) tortilla. Repeat with the remaining dough balls.

Heat a griddle or cast-iron skillet over medium-high heat.

Place 4 to 6 tortillas onto the hot griddle and cook for 30 seconds, then flip and cook for another 30 seconds, or until the tortilla looks cooked and the edges are slightly browned.

Transfer the tortilla to a tortilla warmer or wrap it in a tea towel to keep warm; it will soften as it sits. Repeat the process with the remaining tortillas and serve warm.

Wrap leftover tortillas in plastic wrap, a zip-top bag, or an airtight container and store in the refrigerator for up to 1 week. Reheat in a toaster oven or on a griddle. They are delicious for breakfast or dessert with a little butter, a sprinkle of ground cinnamon, and a touch of sugar or honey.

LAURA'S TIP: You'll find masa harina (finely ground cornmeal) near the Mexican ingredients at your grocery store.

GRAIN-FREE TORTILLAS

....

YIELD: 8 TORTILLAS

This recipe made its debut appearance in my third cookbook, *The Best Grain-Free Family Meals on the Planet*. No taco book would be complete without an alternative to the original corn tortilla. They are really delicious!

1 packed cup (118 g) almond flour
½ packed cup (65 g) tapioca flour
¼ teaspoon ground cumin (optional)

¼ teaspoon sea salt
3 tablespoons (45 ml) avocado oil or olive oil
3 tablespoons (45 ml) warm water

In a medium bowl, whisk together the almond flour, tapioca flour, cumin (if using), and salt to combine.

Add the oil and mix well. Slowly add the water, 1 tablespoon (15 ml) at a time, and knead with your hands to combine.

Transfer the dough to your work surface and knead for about a minute to combine. If the dough is too wet, add a little more almond flour. If it is too dry, add a teaspoon or two of water. The dough texture will vary depending on how you measure the flours; see my note below.

Heat a griddle or cast-iron skillet over medium-high heat. While the griddle is heating, use your hands to form 8 equal-size dough balls.

Place a dough ball between two pieces of parchment paper. If you are using a tortilla press, simply press down to flatten. If you are using a rolling pin, roll the dough into a thin, 6-inch (15 cm) tortilla.

Peel off the top parchment and flip the tortilla onto the hot pan, pulling away the second piece of parchment paper as you do. Cook the first side for about 20 seconds, until it begins to brown. Flip the tortilla and cook the other side for 30 to 45 seconds, until the other side is browned and bubbly.

Transfer the tortilla to a tortilla warmer or wrap it in a tea towel to keep warm. Repeat with the remaining dough balls.

These tortillas are best served warm. Wrap leftover tortillas in plastic wrap and store in the refrigerator for up to 1 week. To enjoy again, simply warm them in the toaster oven.

‖‖‖‖‖‖‖‖‖‖‖‖‖‖‖‖‖‖‖‖‖‖‖‖‖‖‖‖‖

LAURA'S TIP: Use a large griddle for these if you have one, because it can cook 4 to 6 tortillas at a time. Working quickly is a must because they are most pliable when warm.

FLOUR TORTILLAS

YIELD: 12 TO 15 TORTILLAS

Soft and full of air bubbles that hug taco fillings well, these tortillas are as authentic as they get. Thank you, Carmen, for sharing your abuelita's recipe.

3 cups (375 g) all-purpose flour
2 teaspoons baking powder
1 teaspoon salt
¼ cup (50 g) lard or vegetable shortening
1¼ cups (295 ml) warm water

In a mixing bowl, whisk together the flour, baking powder, and salt. Mix in the lard with your fingers until the mixture resembles coarse sand. Add the water and mix until the dough comes together.

Transfer the dough to a lightly floured surface and knead for a few minutes, until smooth, dusting with a very small amount of flour if the dough is too sticky.

Divide the dough into 12 to 15 equal-size pieces and roll each piece into a ball.

Preheat a large skillet, preferably cast iron, over medium-high heat. While the skillet is heating up, use a well-floured rolling pin to roll one dough ball into a thin, 8-inch (20 cm) tortilla. Or use a tortilla press to flatten the dough between two pieces of parchment paper. Then peel off the parchment and flip the tortilla into the hot pan, peeling off the second piece of parchment as you do.

Place the tortilla in the hot skillet and cook until bubbly and brown in spots on the bottom. Flip and continue to cook for an additional minute, until more bubbles and golden spots appear. Transfer the tortilla to a tortilla warmer or wrap it in a tea towel to keep warm.

Repeat the process with the remaining dough balls and serve warm.

Wrap leftover tortillas in plastic wrap, a zip-top bag, or an airtight container and store in the refrigerator for up to 1 week. Reheat in a toaster oven or skillet.

BAKED TOSTADAS

YIELD: 8 TOSTADAS

I prefer a tostada when I want to load up my taco with a lot of something saucy or top it with a fried egg. Sometimes you just don't want to squeeze your stuffing, you know?

8 (6-inch/15 cm) corn tortillas, store-bought or
   homemade (page 32)
3 tablespoons (45 ml) vegetable oil

Preheat the oven to 350°F (180°C).

Brush the corn tortillas on both sides with oil and place on a baking sheet. Bake for about 5 minutes per side, until golden brown and crispy. Serve warm.

LAURA'S TIPS: You can also fry these in a skillet, if preferred.

Leftover tostadas can be stored in an airtight container for up to 3 days. To reheat, toast them up in the toaster oven.

PERFECT PANCAKES

YIELD: 10 PANCAKES

In my cookbook *The Best Homemade Kids' Lunches on the Planet* and on my websites, this recipe has been viewed by millions. It's a classic and it makes a great shell for a breakfast taco.

1½ cups (188 g) all-purpose flour
3½ teaspoons (16 g) baking powder
1 tablespoon (13 g) sugar
1 teaspoon (6 g) salt
1¼ cups (295 ml) milk
1 large egg
3 tablespoons (42 g) unsalted butter, melted,
   plus more for cooking

In a large bowl, sift together the flour, baking powder, sugar, and salt. Pour in the milk, egg, and melted butter; mix with a fork until smooth.

Heat a nonstick griddle or large nonstick skillet over medium-high heat (375°F or 190°C) and grease with butter.

Ladle out ¼ cup (60 ml) of batter for each pancake. Using the back of the ladle, make a circular motion to spread the batter into a thin tortilla (omit this step if you prefer thick, fluffy pancakes). Cook for 3 minutes on the first side, or until bubbles form on top, then flip. Cook the other side until golden brown. Transfer to a plate and repeat the process with the remaining batter.

Refrigerate leftover pancakes in plastic wrap for up to 1 week. Reheat in a toaster oven or skillet.

SRIRACHA-LIKE SEASONING

YIELD: ABOUT $\frac{1}{3}$ CUP (40 G)

You've hit the lottery with this one, my friends. It adds a little spicy dust to any food—not just tacos, but also scrambled eggs, plain fish, and anywhere else you want to turn up the heat.

25 small dried red chiles (such as chiles de árbol)
1 tablespoon (15 g) brown sugar
2 teaspoons sea salt
½ teaspoon garlic powder

With a paring knife, slice each chile in half, scrape out the seeds, and discard the seeds.

In a small food processor or spice grinder, pulverize the red chiles, a few at a time, until they are finely ground. Add the brown sugar, sea salt, and garlic powder and finely grind again.

Transfer to an airtight container and store at room temperature for up to 2 months.

LAURA'S TIP: Either use food-safe gloves when handling chiles or avoid touching your eyes or face, and be sure to wash your hands thoroughly after handling them.

ARRIBA! SEASONING ›

YIELD: ABOUT ½ CUP (60 G)

This is the ultimate taco seasoning, my holy grail of all-purpose seasonings. I have shared it in two previous cookbooks and I'm thrilled to share it again with you here. When in doubt, sprinkle it over *everything*.

3 tablespoons (23 g) chili powder
2 tablespoons (14 g) ground cumin
1 tablespoon (7 g) paprika
1½ teaspoons salt
2 teaspoons freshly ground black pepper
2 teaspoons dried oregano
2 teaspoons garlic powder
1 teaspoon onion powder

In a small bowl, whisk together all the seasonings. Store in an airtight container at room temperature for up to 6 months.

CHAPTER 2

TACOS, TACOS, TACOS!

The recipes in the following sections
are all you need to make Taco Tuesday
the best meal of your week—guaranteed.

BLACK BEANS AND QUESO BREAKFAST TACOS

YIELD: 4 SERVINGS

Breakfast for dinner just got better with these basic and yet super delicious tacos. You'll find Cotija cheese in the refrigerated section of the grocery store, although in a pinch you can substitute goat cheese.

1 tablespoon (15 ml) vegetable oil
6 large eggs
1 can (15-ounce/428 g) black beans, rinsed and drained
8 corn tortillas, store-bought or homemade (page 32), warmed
4 ounces (115 g) Cotija cheese, crumbled
1 avocado, pitted, peeled, and sliced
Chopped fresh cilantro

In a large skillet, heat the oil over medium-high heat and scramble the eggs. Meanwhile, in a small saucepan, warm up the beans over medium-low heat.

Distribute the eggs evenly over the tortillas, top with some black beans, then sprinkle on some cheese. Top with avocado slices and finely chopped cilantro and serve immediately.

BREAKFAST OF CHAMPIONS TACOS

YIELD: 4 SERVINGS

Here's an unconventional taco with a fun and tasty twist. This classic breakfast combination is the ultimate kid-friendly take on a breakfast taco. If you don't have kids, pretend that you do, because not making these would be a real tragedy.

6 ounces (170 g) sausage, crumbled
8 large eggs
8 Perfect Pancakes (page 37), warmed
⅓ cup (80 ml) maple syrup

In a large skillet, cook the sausage over medium-high heat until cooked through. Pour off the grease. Add the eggs and scramble them with the sausage.

To assemble, place a pancake on a taco holder or hold it folded in your hand, top with scrambled eggs and sausage, and drizzle a little maple syrup on top. Serve immediately.

BREAKFAST SAUSAGE AND PINEAPPLE SALSA TACOS

....

YIELD: 4 SERVINGS

Making these breakfast tacos is fun and easy. Starting with fully cooked sausage makes for an ultra-convenient breakfast for those days when we are in a rush.

8 (1-ounce/28 g) fully cooked turkey breakfast sausage patties
2 cups (60 g) baby spinach, chopped
8 flour tortillas, store-bought or homemade (page 36), warmed
Pineapple Salsa (page 23)

Heat up the sausage patties according to the package directions.

Scatter some baby spinach on each tortilla and top with a heaping tablespoon of fresh pineapple salsa.

Place a sausage patty on each taco, either cut in half or whole, fold, and enjoy immediately.

HUEVOS VERDES TACOS

YIELD: 4 SERVINGS

This is a perfect way to use up any Salsa Verde (page 24) and Cilantro-Lime Dressing (page 28) you might have left over from a previous taco night. Yes, that implies having two taco nights in one week, but who's counting?

1 tablespoon (15 ml) vegetable oil
8 large eggs, whisked
¼ cup (30 g) shredded cheddar cheese, plus extra for topping
8 corn tortillas, store-bought or homemade (page 32), warmed
Salsa Verde (page 24)
Cilantro-Lime Dressing (page 28)

In a large skillet, heat the oil over medium heat. Add the eggs and scramble until almost cooked through. Add the shredded cheddar and finish cooking the eggs.

Divide the scrambled eggs atop the corn tortillas, top with some salsa verde and cilantro-lime dressing, and finish with a sprinkle of shredded cheese. Serve immediately.

HUEVOS RANCHEROS TACOS

YIELD: 4 SERVINGS

May I present: the traditional Mexican breakfast inside a taco. Because all great things deserve to be inside a taco! Be sure to have all your ingredients prepped and ready before heating your tortillas so these will come together in a flash.

8 corn tortillas, store-bought or homemade (page 32)
1 can (15-ounce/428 g) black beans, rinsed and drained
½ cup (60 g) shredded Mexican blend cheese
2 teaspoons olive oil
8 large eggs
¼ teaspoon freshly ground black pepper
½ cup (120 g) Pico de Gallo (page 23)
Sour cream
½ avocado, peeled and diced
¼ cup (4 g) chopped fresh cilantro
1 lime, cut into wedges

Place an oven rack in the middle position and preheat the broiler to low.

Spread out the tortillas on a baking sheet and coat with cooking spray. Broil for 2 minutes. Remove the baking sheet from the oven and flip the tortillas over so the toasted side is face down.

Divide the black beans among the tortillas and sprinkle with cheese. Return the baking sheet to the oven and broil for 1 to 2 minutes, until the cheese is melted. Remove the baking sheet from the oven and place it next to the stovetop.

In a large nonstick skillet, heat the oil over medium-high heat. Crack two eggs into the skillet and cook until the whites are cooked through, then flip. Transfer each egg to one of the tortillas, on top of the black beans and cheese. Repeat with the remaining eggs. Sprinkle with the pepper.

Top the tacos with 1 tablespoon (15 g) pico de gallo, sour cream, avocado, and cilantro. Serve with lime wedges.

MIGAS BREAKFAST TACOS

YIELD: 4 SERVINGS

Migas is the classic Tex-Mex breakfast. Usually it's served with tortillas alongside, but of course I like to serve it taco style!

1 tablespoon (15 ml) olive oil
½ cup (130 g) Pico de Gallo (page 23)
8 large eggs, beaten
½ cup (25 g) roughly crushed tortilla chips
½ cup (60 g) shredded cheddar cheese, plus more for serving
8 corn tortillas, store-bought or homemade (page 32), warmed
1 avocado, pitted, peeled, and sliced
Chopped fresh cilantro

In a large skillet, the heat the oil over medium-high heat. Add the pico de gallo and cook, stirring, for about 4 minutes, until the onion has softened. Pour the eggs into the skillet and cook. Add the tortilla chips and shredded cheese, toss to combine, and remove from the heat.

Divide the cooked egg mixture over the corn tortillas, sprinkle with additional cheese, and top with avocado slices and cilantro.

BACON AND EGG BREAKFAST TACOS

YIELD: 4 SERVINGS

No breakfast menu is complete without bacon, and these bacon and egg breakfast tacos are as delicious as they sound.

1 tablespoon (15 ml) vegetable oil
8 eggs, whisked
Pinch salt
½ cup (60 g) shredded cheddar cheese
8 corn tortillas, store-bought or homemade (page 32), warmed
4 slices bacon, cooked and coarsely chopped
1 cup (150 g) cherry tomatoes, halved
1 avocado, pitted, peeled, and diced
Chopped fresh cilantro

In a large skillet, heat the oil over medium-high heat. Add the eggs and salt and scramble the eggs until cooked through. Sprinkle the cheese on top and remove from the heat.

Divide the scrambled eggs among the tortillas and top with some chopped bacon, cherry tomatoes, and diced avocado. Sprinkle with cilantro and serve.

STEAK AND EGG TACOS

YIELD: 4 SERVINGS

The classic diner breakfast reinvented inside a taco. This hearty meal is one you'll want to make on the weekends for breakfast, too!

2 tablespoons (30 ml) vegetable oil, divided
1 bag (12-ounce/340 g) frozen fajita vegetable mix
8 ounces (225 g) deli roast beef, finely chopped
8 large eggs, whisked
Pinch salt
1 can (15-ounce/428 g) black beans, rinsed and drained
8 flour tortillas, store-bought or homemade (page 36), warmed
1 avocado, pitted, peeled, and sliced
½ cup (75 g) crumbled Cotija cheese
Chopped fresh cilantro
Restaurant-Style Salsa (page 20)

In a large skillet, heat 1 tablespoon (15 ml) of the oil over medium-high heat. Add the fajita mix to the skillet and cook, stirring, until the vegetables soften, 5 to 7 minutes. Add the roast beef and cook for 3 minutes. Transfer the vegetables and roast beef to a plate.

Heat the remaining 1 tablespoon (15 ml) oil in the same skillet and scramble the eggs with a pinch of salt until cooked through.

Meanwhile, heat the black beans in a small saucepan over medium-low heat or in the microwave.

Divide the beef and vegetable mixture among the tortillas, top them with scrambled eggs and black beans, and add some avocado and Cotija cheese. Garnish with cilantro and serve with salsa.

LAURA'S TIPS: Instead of scrambling the eggs, you can cook them sunny-side up and place one on the taco mixture. Can't find fajita mix in the freezer section? Slice 2 medium bell peppers and 1 small onion instead.

BLACKENED ZUCCHINI TACOS

....

YIELD: 4 SERVINGS

These tacos have "summer" written all over them. They are perfect for when you want a light meal or you have an abundance of zucchinis and you don't know what else to make with them.

2 tablespoons (30 ml) extra virgin olive oil, divided
2 medium zucchinis, cut into ½-inch (1.3 cm) slices
1½ tablespoons (12 g) Arriba! Seasoning (page 38), divided
1 medium red onion, diced
¾ cup (98 g) corn
1 can (15-ounce/428 g) black beans, rinsed and drained
8 corn tortillas, store-bought or homemade (page 32), warmed
Easy Pickled Jalapeños and Onions (page 24)
½ cup (75 g) crumbled Cotija cheese
1 lime, cut into wedges

In a large skillet, heat 1½ tablespoons (22 ml) of the olive oil over medium-high heat. Add the zucchini slices and sprinkle with half of the seasoning. Flip and cook on the other side. Transfer to a plate and cover to keep warm.

Reduce the heat to medium and add the remaining ½ tablespoon (8 ml) oil. Add the onion and the remaining seasoning and sauté for about 5 minutes, until the onion has softened. Add the corn and stir to heat through.

Meanwhile, heat the black beans in a small saucepan over medium-low heat or in the microwave.

Assemble each tortilla by starting with a layer of onion, then a layer of zucchini slices, and then some pickled jalapeños. Top with crumbled Cotija cheese and serve with lime wedges.

BUFFALO CHICKPEA LETTUCE CUPS

YIELD: 6 SERVINGS

Have you ever purchased a bottle of buffalo sauce for a recipe and then kept what's left sitting in your fridge, waiting to be used again? Well, here's your solution: a recipe soon to be devoured by your entire family that can be made into a traditional taco or served inside a crispy base of iceberg lettuce. Homemade ranch dressing included.

½ cup (115 g) mayonnaise

¼ cup (60 ml) milk

2 tablespoons (8 g) finely chopped fresh parsley

1 teaspoon dried dill

1 teaspoon garlic powder

Pinch salt and freshly ground black pepper

1 tablespoon (15 ml) vegetable oil

1 small onion, finely chopped

2 cans (14-ounce/428 g) chickpeas, rinsed and drained

½ cup (120 ml) buffalo sauce

1 head iceberg, Boston Bibb, or other leafy lettuce, leaves separated

1 avocado, pitted, peeled, and sliced

4 ounces (112 g) crumbled blue cheese

Chopped fresh cilantro or parsley

To make the homemade ranch dressing, in a medium bowl, whisk together the mayonnaise, milk, parsley, dill, garlic powder, salt, and pepper. Cover and refrigerate while you make the tacos (can be made up to 5 days ahead of time).

In a large skillet, heat the oil over medium-high heat. Sauté the onion for about 5 minutes, until it turns golden and translucent. Add the chickpeas and continue to cook, stirring frequently, for another 2 to 3 minutes. Add the buffalo sauce, reduce the heat to a simmer, and cook, stirring, for 3 minutes to heat through.

Layer two lettuce leaves to build each cup and scoop ⅓ cup (80 g) of the chickpea mixture into it. Drizzle with the ranch, sprinkle on some blue cheese, and top with avocado slices. Garnish with fresh herbs.

LAURA'S TIP: You can, of course, use your favorite store-bought ranch dressing for this recipe.

CURRIED CAULIFLOWER TACOS WITH PINEAPPLE SALSA

YIELD: 4 SERVINGS

Who knew cauliflower could be such a delicious addition to tacos? Roasted cauliflower seasoned with curry and turmeric, plus fresh homemade salsa: This is a taco recipe nobody should miss.

3 tablespoons (45 ml) olive oil
1 tablespoon (6 g) curry powder
1 cauliflower, cut into small florets
8 corn tortillas, store-bought or homemade (page 32), warmed
Pineapple Salsa (page 23)
Sour cream (optional)

Preheat the oven to 375°F (190°C).

In a large bowl, combine the olive oil and curry powder. Add the cauliflower florets and toss to combine. Transfer the cauliflower to a 13 × 9-inch (33 × 23 cm) glass baking dish.

Roast the cauliflower for about 30 minutes, until the tops begin to turn golden brown, tossing after about 20 minutes.

Stuff the tortillas with the cauliflower and top with pineapple salsa and a drizzle of sour cream, if desired.

CHICKPEA AND BUTTERNUT SQUASH TACOS

YIELD: 4 SERVINGS

These simple, budget-friendly tacos work just as well for Meatless Monday as Taco Tuesday! You'll fall in love with the combination of crispy chickpeas and creamy butternut squash.

1 tablespoon (7 g) taco seasoning
3 tablespoons (45 ml) lime juice (1 to 2 limes), divided
1 tablespoon (15 ml) olive oil
1 tablespoon (15 ml) water
1 can (15-ounce/428 g) chickpeas, rinsed and drained
1 pound (454 g) diced butternut squash, thawed if frozen
1 cup (230 g) plain Greek yogurt or sour cream
¼ cup (4 g) chopped fresh cilantro
Salt and freshly ground black pepper, to taste
8 corn tortillas, store-bought or homemade (page 32), warmed
1 cup (70 g) finely chopped red cabbage
1 jalapeño, seeded and sliced
1 large avocado, pitted, peeled, and diced
1 lime, cut into wedges

Preheat the oven to 400°F (200°C) and line a rimmed baking sheet with parchment paper.

In a large bowl, combine the taco seasoning, 1 tablespoon (15 ml) of the lime juice, olive oil, and water. Add the chickpeas and squash cubes and toss to coat well.

Transfer the seasoned chickpeas and squash to the prepared baking sheet. Roast for 30 to 35 minutes, stirring occasionally, until the chickpeas are slightly crispy and the squash is tender.

Meanwhile, in a small bowl, whisk together the Greek yogurt, remaining 2 tablespoons (30 ml) lime juice, and cilantro. Stir well. Season with salt and pepper.

To assemble each taco, start with a warm tortilla and top with a bed of cabbage, roasted chickpeas, squash, jalapeños, and avocado. Drizzle on some cilantro-lime sauce and serve with additional lime wedges.

POBLANO PEPPER AND MUSHROOM TACOS

YIELD: 4 SERVINGS

I first tried these while camping with friends, where they cooked everything in a cast-iron skillet. Whenever I make them at home, I double the recipe for good measure and use the leftovers to top a bed of romaine lettuce later in the week for an out-of-this-world lunch salad drizzled with the cilantro-lime dressing.

1 bunch kale, roughly chopped
2 limes, juiced, divided
Pinch salt
1 cup (165 g) diced fresh pineapple
1 jalapeño, seeded and chopped, divided
¾ cup (12 g) chopped fresh cilantro, divided
2 tablespoons (30 ml) vegetable oil
1 red onion, diced
2 poblano peppers, seeded and sliced
4 garlic cloves, grated
1 pound (454 g) cremini or button mushrooms, sliced
2 tablespoons (15 g) Arriba! Seasoning (page 38)
8 corn tortillas, store-bought or homemade (page 32), warmed
Cilantro-Lime Dressing (page 28)
1 avocado, pitted, peeled, and sliced (optional)

In a large bowl, massage the kale for a minute or two with the juice of 1 lime and a pinch of salt. Add the pineapple, half of the chopped jalapeño, and half of the chopped cilantro.

In a large cast-iron skillet, heat the oil over medium-high heat. Add the onion and cook for 5 minutes, or until soft. Add the peppers, garlic, and remaining jalapeño and cook for 3 minutes, or until the peppers begin to soften. Add the mushrooms and seasoning and cook for an additional 3 minutes.

To serve, place a bed of the kale-pineapple mixture on each tortilla, top with the veggie mixture, and drizzle with dressing. Serve with sliced avocado, the remaining cilantro, and lime wedges on the side, if desired.

ORANGE-GLAZED MUSHROOM TACOS WITH VEGGIE SLAW

YIELD: 4 SERVINGS

In this recipe, the best of Asian fusion food comes in our favorite vessel: a taco! One bite and you'll know why these tacos are the real deal.

3 tablespoons (45 g) orange marmalade
1 tablespoon (15 ml) soy sauce
1 inch (2.5 cm) piece ginger, peeled and grated
1 small garlic clove, grated
¾ teaspoon five-spice powder
1½ cups (105 g) shredded red cabbage
1 cup (110 g) carrot matchsticks
½ cucumber, julienned
3 scallions, sliced diagonally
1 tablespoon (15 ml) toasted sesame oil
2 large portobello mushrooms, stemmed and sliced into strips
1 teaspoon sesame seeds
8 corn tortillas, store-bought or homemade (page 32), warmed
1 lime, cut into wedges

In a small bowl, whisk together the orange marmalade, soy sauce, ginger, garlic, and five-spice powder. Set aside.

In a medium bowl, combine the cabbage, carrots, cucumber, and scallions. Set aside.

In a large skillet, heat the sesame oil over medium-high heat. Add the sliced mushrooms and cook, stirring, for 2 to 3 minutes. Once the mushroom slices have begun to soften and brown, pour the orange sauce into the pan and stir to combine. Reduce the heat to low and cook for 1 minute for the sauce to reduce. Stir in the sesame seeds and remove the pan from the heat.

To serve, place a bed of veggies on each tortilla, top with orange-glazed mushrooms, and squeeze a lime wedge on top.

SOUTHWESTERN TACOS

YIELD: 4 SERVINGS

This is one of my favorite recipes to cook when I'm exhausted after a long day of work or pressed for time. The veggies are easy to prep ahead, so all I have to do is spread them out on a baking pan and the oven does all the work.

1 pint (300 g) cherry tomatoes, halved
1½ cups (195 g) corn
3 medium zucchinis or yellow summer squash, diced
½ onion, sliced
1 red bell pepper, seeded and sliced
2 tablespoons (30 ml) olive oil
1 tablespoon (7 g) Arriba! Seasoning (page 38)
1 can (15-ounce/428 g) black beans, rinsed and drained
1 lime, cut into wedges
8 corn tortillas, store-bought or homemade (page 32), warmed
Crumbled goat cheese or Cotija cheese
⅓ cup (5 g) chopped fresh cilantro

Position an oven rack in the middle of the oven and preheat the oven to 400°F (200°C). Line a rimmed baking sheet with parchment paper.

In a large bowl, combine the tomatoes, corn, zucchinis, onion, and pepper. Add the olive oil and seasoning and toss so that all the veggies are evenly coated. Transfer to the prepared baking sheet.

Roast the veggies for 10 minutes, then stir and continue to roast for another 5 minutes. Add the black beans and squeeze a few lime wedges on top, stir, and roast for 5 to 10 more minutes, until all the veggies are soft.

To serve, spoon some roasted veggies onto each tortilla, top with crumbled cheese, and sprinkle cilantro on top. Serve with additional lime wedges.

CHIPOTLE BEET AND EGG TOSTADAS

YIELD: 4 SERVINGS

I love the roasted beet and goat cheese combination on this crispy, flat shell. The sweet and savory really come through, with a little kick from the chipotles. The fried egg just takes this tostada over the top.

4 medium beets, ends trimmed
1 can (7-ounce/196 g) chipotle peppers in adobo sauce
2 tablespoons (30 ml) vegetable oil, divided
¼ teaspoon ground cumin
¼ teaspoon salt
1 lime, halved, divided
4 large eggs
8 Baked Tostadas (page 37), freshly made or re-crisped in the oven
6 ounces (175 g) goat cheese, crumbled
Chopped fresh cilantro

Preheat the oven to 375°F (190°C).

Place each beet in the middle of a square of aluminum foil. Pour some adobo sauce from the canned chipotles over each beet; reserve the chipotles. Wrap the beets and place on a baking sheet. Roast for about 50 minutes, until fork tender. Remove the beets from the oven and let them cool to room temperature for about 10 minutes.

Carefully open the foil packets. Peel and cube the beets.

Coarsely chop the chipotle peppers.

In a large skillet, heat 1 tablespoon (15 ml) of the oil over medium-high heat. Add the beets, chipotles, cumin, salt, and the juice of half a lime. Stir gently to combine and heat through for about 3 minutes. Set aside.

In another large skillet, heat the remaining 1 tablespoon (15 ml) oil over medium heat and cook the eggs sunny-side up.

Make a layer of beets and chipotles on each tostada, top with goat cheese crumbles, add a fried egg, and sprinkle with cilantro. Cut the remaining lime half into wedges for serving.

BUFFALO CHICKEN TACOS WITH HOMEMADE RANCH

YIELD: 6 SERVINGS

Everything you love about buffalo chicken wings—inside a taco.

½ cup (115 g) mayonnaise
¼ cup (60 ml) milk
2 tablespoons (8 g) finely chopped fresh parsley
1 teaspoon dried dill
1 teaspoon garlic powder
Pinch salt and freshly ground black pepper
1 tablespoon (15 ml) vegetable oil
1 small onion, finely chopped
1½ pounds (680 g) boneless, skinless chicken breasts, cut into bite-size chunks
½ cup (120 ml) buffalo sauce
8 corn tortillas, store-bought or homemade (page 32), warmed
4 ounces (115 g) blue cheese crumbles
1 avocado, pitted, peeled, and sliced

To make the homemade ranch dressing, in a medium bowl, whisk together the mayonnaise, milk, parsley, dill, garlic powder, salt, and pepper. Cover and refrigerate while you make the tacos (can be made up to 5 days ahead of time).

In a large skillet, heat the oil over medium-high heat. Sauté the onion for about 5 minutes, until it turns golden and translucent. Add the chicken and cook, stirring frequently, for 5 minutes, or until the chicken is cooked through. Stir in the buffalo sauce, reduce the heat to a simmer, and cook, stirring, for 3 minutes to heat through.

To assemble, scoop ⅓ cup (75 g) of the chicken mixture on top of each tortilla, top with blue cheese and avocado slices, and drizzle with ranch.

JAMAICAN JERK CHICKEN TACOS

YIELD: 4 SERVINGS

These tacos are great the day of, but my favorite might be turning the leftovers into a chicken taco salad by placing them on top of a bed of romaine lettuce.

⅓ cup (77 g) sour cream
½ lime, juiced
1 tablespoon (7 g) + 2 teaspoons (5 g) Jamaican jerk seasoning, divided
1½ pounds (680 g) boneless, skinless chicken breasts, cut into thin strips
2 tablespoons (30 ml) vegetable oil
1½ cups (250 g) chopped fresh pineapple
2 cups (140 g) purple and green shredded cabbage
8 corn tortillas, store-bought or homemade (page 32), warmed
3 tablespoons (21 g) chopped fresh cilantro

In a small bowl, whisk together the sour cream, lime juice, and 2 teaspoons (5 g) of the jerk seasoning. Cover and refrigerate while you make the tacos.

In a large bowl, toss the chicken strips with the remaining 1 tablespoon (7 g) jerk seasoning to coat evenly.

In a large skillet, heat the oil over medium-high heat. Add the seasoned chicken and cook for 5 to 7 minutes, until cooked through. Use a slotted spoon or tongs to transfer the chicken to a plate and cover with another plate to keep warm.

Add the chopped pineapple to the skillet and cook with the leftover seasoning and tidbits in the pan for 3 to 4 minutes, until the pineapple is browned and its juices have begun to break down. Remove the pan from the heat, return the chicken to the pan, and toss to combine.

To assemble the tacos, make a bed of cabbage on each tortilla, top with a scoop of the chicken and pineapple mixture, drizzle some jerk cream sauce on top, and sprinkle with cilantro.

SLOW COOKER CHICKEN SALSA VERDE TACOS

YIELD: 6 SERVINGS

There's nothing better than a sweet and spicy taco with the classic salsa verde flavors we all love. Pile the ingredients into a taco shell and you'll soon be saying, "Ay, Dios mío, give me more!"

2 pounds (1 kg) boneless, skinless chicken breasts
1 cup (260 g) Salsa Verde (page 24)
½ cup (170 g) honey
½ cup (120 ml) lime juice (about 4 limes)
2 tablespoons (15 g) Arriba! Seasoning (page 38)
8 crunchy corn taco shells, warmed
1½ cups (180 g) shredded Monterey Jack cheese
1½ cups (80 g) shredded romaine lettuce
Pico de Gallo (page 23)
1 avocado, pitted, peeled, and diced

Put the chicken breasts in a slow cooker and top with the salsa verde, honey, lime juice, and seasoning.

Cover and cook on high for 4 to 5 hours or on low for 8 hours, or until the meat separates easily with a fork.

Transfer the chicken breasts to a cutting board and use two forks to shred the meat. Return the shredded chicken to the slow cooker, cover, and cook for an additional 30 minutes to allow the meat to absorb the sauce and seasonings.

Using tongs, transfer the chicken to a serving platter, leaving the excess liquid in the slow cooker.

Stuff each taco shell with chicken and top with cheese, lettuce, pico de gallo, and avocado.

SWEET AND SPICY SRIRACHA CHICKEN TACOS

YIELD: 4 SERVINGS

You'll love the explosion of flavors of this marinated grilled chicken topped with avocado, lettuce, cilantro sour cream, and honey-Sriracha.

1½ pounds (680 g) boneless, skinless chicken breasts

4 tablespoons (60 g) Sriracha sauce, divided

1 tablespoon (20 g) + 2 teaspoons (14 g) honey, divided

2 limes, juiced, divided

½ cup (115 g) sour cream

1½ tablespoons (4g) finely chopped fresh cilantro

¼ teaspoon salt

1½ tablespoons (22 ml) vegetable oil (if not using a grill)

2 cups (110 g) shredded romaine lettuce

1 cup (120 g) shredded cheddar cheese

1 avocado, pitted, peeled, and sliced

8 corn tortillas, store-bought or homemade (page 32), warmed

Put the chicken breasts in an airtight container or zip-top plastic bag. Add 3 tablespoons (45 g) of the Sriracha, 1 tablespoon (20 g) of the honey, and the juice of 1 lime. Mix to combine, seal, and refrigerate for at least 4 hours or overnight.

In a small bowl, whisk together the sour cream, remaining juice of 1 lime, cilantro, and salt. Cover and refrigerate while you make the tacos.

In a small bowl, whisk together the remaining 1 tablespoon (15 g) Sriracha and remaining 2 teaspoons (14 g) honey and set aside.

Preheat a grill or heat the oil in a large skillet over medium-high heat. Remove the chicken breasts from the marinade and cook for 5 to 7 minutes, flip, and cook on the other side for 5 minutes, or until the internal temperature reaches 165°F (73°C).

Transfer the chicken to a plate and rest until cool enough to handle. With two forks, shred the chicken.

Assemble the tacos by layering the chicken, lettuce, cheese, and avocado on the tortillas. Drizzle the cilantro sour cream on top and finish with a single drizzle of spicy honey-Sriracha sauce.

TERIYAKI CHICKEN TACOS

YIELD: 6 SERVINGS

One of my kids' favorite sauces turned into a taco! I couldn't help but create a grown-up version with the sweet, grilled pineapple salsa.

½ cup (115 g) plain yogurt
1 cup (165 g) fresh pineapple chunks, divided
½ lime, juiced
⅛ teaspoon cayenne pepper (optional)
1½ pounds (680 g) boneless, skinless chicken breasts, sliced into strips
1 cup (240 ml) teriyaki sauce, divided
1 tablespoon (15 ml) vegetable oil
2 cups (110 g) shredded romaine lettuce
1½ cups (180 g) shredded Monterey Jack cheese
12 flour tortillas, store-bought or homemade (page 36), warmed

In a blender, blend the yogurt, ½ cup (85 g) of the pineapple chunks, juice of ½ lime, and cayenne pepper (if using) until smooth. Transfer to an airtight container and refrigerate for up to 3 days.

Put the chicken breast strips in an airtight container or zip-top plastic bag. Add ½ cup (120 ml) of the teriyaki sauce, seal, and toss to combine. Refrigerate for at least 4 hours or up to overnight.

In a large cast-iron skillet, heat the oil over medium-high heat. Remove the chicken from the marinade and cook for about 5 minutes, flip, and cook on the other side for 7 minutes, or until cooked through. Remove the pan from the heat, add the remaining ½ cup (120 ml) teriyaki sauce, and toss to coat the chicken. Transfer the chicken to a plate.

Assemble the tacos by layering the shredded lettuce, cheese, teriyaki chicken, and remaining ½ cup (85 g) pineapple chunks on the tortillas. Drizzle the creamy pineapple sauce over the top.

SLOW COOKER THAI CHICKEN LETTUCE CUPS

....

YIELD: 6 SERVINGS

This delicious recipe is my favorite way to eat more vegetables. Whether you serve the chicken inside a lettuce cup or a tortilla, you'll love the crunchy texture.

CHICKEN

¼ cup (60 ml) lime juice (about 2 limes)
¼ cup (60 ml) soy sauce
3 tablespoons (60 g) honey
2 tablespoons (30 ml) vegetable oil
1 tablespoon (15 ml) fish sauce
2 teaspoons (10 ml) Sriracha sauce

4 garlic cloves, grated
2 teaspoons (10 g) grated fresh ginger
2 scallions, chopped, green parts reserved
  for the tacos
1½ pounds (680 g) boneless, skinless chicken
  breasts, cut into halves or thirds

ASSEMBLY

1 cup (70 g) shredded purple cabbage
1 cup (110 g) carrot matchsticks
1 cup (150 g) diced red bell pepper
⅓ cup (50 g) chopped unsalted peanuts

½ cup (8 g) chopped fresh cilantro
1 or 2 Boston Bibb lettuce heads, leaves separated
Thai Peanut Sauce (page 31)

TO MAKE THE CHICKEN: In the slow cooker, whisk together the lime juice, soy sauce, honey, oil, fish sauce, Sriracha, garlic, ginger, and white parts of the scallions. Add the chicken and stir to coat with the sauce. Cover and cook on high for 4 hours or on low for 8 hours.

When cooked, transfer the chicken breasts to a cutting board and use two forks to shred the meat.

TO ASSEMBLE: In a large bowl, combine the shredded chicken, cabbage, carrot, bell pepper, peanuts, green parts of the scallions, and cilantro.

Layer two lettuce leaves to build each cup and scoop the chicken and veggie mixture into it. Drizzle with peanut sauce.

EASY CHICKEN FAJITAS

YIELD: 4 TO 6 SERVINGS

You won't believe how quick and easy it is to prepare everyone's favorite Tex-Mex restaurant dish, especially if you start marinating the chicken the night before.

4 tablespoons (60 ml) vegetable oil, divided
2 tablespoons (30 ml) fresh lemon juice (about ½ lemon)
1½ tablespoons (12 g) Arriba! Seasoning (page 38)
1½ pounds (680 g) boneless, skinless chicken breasts, cut into thin strips
½ medium red bell pepper, julienned
½ medium green bell pepper, julienned
4 scallions, thinly sliced
½ cup (80 g) chopped onion
8 flour tortillas, store-bought or homemade (page 36), warmed
1 cup (120 g) shredded cheddar cheese
Pico de Gallo (page 23)
Easy Guacamole (page 19)
Sour cream

In a large zip-top plastic bag, combine 2 tablespoons (30 ml) of the oil, lemon juice, and seasoning. Add the chicken, seal, and turn to coat. Refrigerate for at least 4 hours or overnight.

In a large skillet, heat the remaining 2 tablespoons (30 ml) oil over medium-high heat. Sauté the bell peppers and onion for 5 to 7 minutes, until crisp-tender. Transfer the vegetables to a plate and cover with another plate to keep warm.

Remove the chicken strips from the marinade and add them to the same skillet. Cook for 3 minutes on the first side, flip, and cook for another 4 minutes, until cooked through. Return the peppers and onion to the skillet and stir to heat through.

Transfer the chicken and pepper mixture to a large platter and bring to the table along with the remaining ingredients in individual serving bowls. Assemble the fajita tacos family style.

BARBECUE CHICKEN TOSTADAS

YIELD: 4 SERVINGS

There's nothing better than turning leftover oven-roasted chicken into tacos. Consider it your taco starter.

3 cups (675 g) shredded cooked chicken
1½ cups (375 g) barbecue sauce, divided
2 cups (240 g) shredded Monterey Jack cheese, divided
8 Baked Tostadas (page 37)
¼ cup (4 g) chopped fresh cilantro
Sour cream

Preheat the oven to 350°F (180°C).

In a large bowl, toss the chicken with 1 cup (250 g) of the barbecue sauce and 1 cup (120 g) of the cheese.

Place the tostadas on a rimmed baking sheet. Distribute the chicken mixture evenly over the tostadas. Bake for 6 to 8 minutes, until the cheese has melted.

Top the tostadas with the remaining 1 cup (120 g) cheese, drizzle with the remaining ½ cup (125 g) barbecue sauce, sprinkle with cilantro, and finish with a dab of sour cream.

CHICKEN ENCHILADA TACOS

YIELD: 4 SERVINGS

My husband loves enchiladas, but I don't always have the time to prepare them, roll them, and then bake them. This version goes from fridge to table in under 20 minutes by taking a few shortcuts—but without sacrificing the traditional enchilada flavors or ingredients. This will become your new way of preparing enchiladas.

1 rotisserie chicken, skin and bones discarded, meat shredded
1 can (8-ounce/235 ml) enchilada sauce
1 cup (120 g) shredded cheddar cheese
1 cup (120 g) shredded Monterey Jack cheese
8 corn tortillas, store-bought or homemade (page 32), warmed
Sour cream
Easy Guacamole (page 19) or Classic Guacamole (page 19)
1 can (4-ounce/115 g) sliced black olives, drained
¼ cup (4 g) chopped fresh cilantro

In a large cast-iron skillet, combine the shredded chicken and enchilada sauce and toss to coat. Bring the mixture to a boil over medium-high heat, reduce the heat to low, and simmer for 3 to 5 minutes, stirring, to heat the chicken through. Remove the pan from the heat.

In a medium bowl, combine the cheeses. Add 1½ cups (180 g) of the cheese to the chicken mixture in the skillet and toss to combine. Cover and set aside for 2 minutes to melt the cheese through while you prepare the remaining ingredients.

Assemble each taco by placing a scoop of the enchilada mixture onto a tortilla and topping with cheese, sour cream, guacamole, sliced olives, and cilantro.

AUNTIE'S MEXICAN CHICKEN TACOS

YIELD: 6 SERVINGS

I first tried this chicken at my Auntie's house in high school. There are no exact measurements for the seasoning, but whatever you do, don't skimp on the salt. Hands down, it is the best roasted chicken recipe I've ever had.

1½ to 2 pounds (680 g to 1 kg) bone-in, skin-on split breasts of chicken
3 tablespoons (55 g) coarse salt
Coarsely ground black pepper
⅓ cup (5 g) Mexican oregano
8 corn tortillas, store-bought or homemade (page 32), warmed
Pico de Gallo (page 23)
1 avocado, pitted, peeled, and sliced
Sour cream

Preheat the oven to 350°F (180°C) and lightly coat a rimmed baking sheet with cooking spray.

Wash the chicken pieces and pat them dry so that the seasoning can adhere. Put the chicken on the prepared baking sheet. Do not remove the skin or bones from the chicken.

Generously salt and pepper the chicken pieces on both sides. Then, generously sprinkle the Mexican oregano all over the chicken.

Bake for 35 to 45 minutes, until the chicken's internal temperature reaches 165°F (73°C). Remove from the oven and allow the chicken to rest for 5 minutes. Remove the skin and bones and shred the meat with two forks or by pulling it apart with your hands.

To assemble the tacos, put some chicken on each tortilla and top with pico de gallo, avocado, and sour cream.

LAURA'S TIP: You'll find dried Mexican oregano by the Latin spices section of most grocery stores. The flavor is very different from regular oregano, so I recommend you use the Mexican variety in this dish.

ALL-AMERICAN BEEF TACOS

YIELD: 6 SERVINGS

No taco book would be complete without this classic, which I like to serve family style. This simple recipe is always a crowd-pleaser—as well as one of my stand-by midweek meals.

1½ pounds (680 g) ground beef
2½ tablespoons (12 g) Arriba! Seasoning (page 38)
12 crunchy corn taco shells, warmed
1½ cups (180 g) shredded cheddar cheese
1½ cups (80 g) shredded iceberg lettuce
Restaurant-Style Salsa (page 20)
Easy Guacamole (page 19)
Sour cream

In a large skillet, cook the meat with the seasoning over medium heat, breaking up the chunks with a wooden spoon into small pieces as it cooks. Once cooked, drain off the fat.

To serve, scoop the beef inside each taco shell and top with the cheese, lettuce, salsa, guacamole, and sour cream.

QUICK CARNE ASADA TACOS

YIELD: 4 SERVINGS

This is a homemade version of the recipe from my local taco shop. Although the traditional version is cooked slowly in the oven, as a busy mom of three kids, I don't always have time for that! This skillet version is much faster and yet has all the rich flavors and juiciness I love from the original in every bite.

1½ teaspoons (4 g) ground cumin
1½ teaspoons (5 g) garlic powder
½ teaspoon kosher salt
Pinch cayenne pepper
4 tablespoons (60 ml) olive oil, divided
1 pound (455 g) skirt steak, sliced into ½-inch
   (1 cm) strips
1 red bell pepper, seeded and sliced

1 green bell pepper, seeded and sliced
1 red onion, sliced
8 corn tortillas, store-bought or homemade
   (page 32), warmed
Sour cream
¼ cup (4 g) chopped fresh cilantro
1 lime, cut into wedges

In a small bowl, combine the cumin, garlic powder, salt, and cayenne with 2 tablespoons (30 ml) of the olive oil.

Pour half of the marinade into a large zip-top bag or airtight container. Add the steak, seal, and toss to combine. Refrigerate for at least 4 hours or overnight.

Pour the remaining marinade into another zip-top bag or airtight container. Add the peppers and onion, seal, and toss to combine. Refrigerate for at least 4 hours or overnight.

In a large cast-iron skillet, heat 1 tablespoon (15 ml) oil over medium heat. Add the steak and cook for 6 to 9 minutes, flipping all the pieces to cook evenly. Transfer the steak to a plate and cover with another plate to keep warm.

Add the remaining 1 tablespoon (15 ml) oil to the skillet and cook the peppers and onion, stirring frequently, for about 7 minutes, until fork tender. Return the steak to the pan and stir for 2 minutes to heat through.

Spoon some of the steak and veggie mixture onto each tortilla. Top with sour cream and cilantro and serve with a lime wedge.

GREEK STEAK TACOS WITH CUCUMBER SALSA

YIELD: 4 TO 6 SERVINGS

Cucumber salsa on a taco with Greek sauce? What happened to Latin tacos? Well, you've clearly never met my stepdad, who is all about Greek everything. Wait until you try this recipe—all those Mediterranean flavors mixed in with a lot of crunchy goodness.

1 small cucumber, finely diced

4 ounces (115 g) Kalamata olives, pitted and chopped

1 cup (150 g) grape tomatoes, halved

1 lime, juiced

½ jalapeño, seeded if desired and minced

1 garlic clove, minced

½ cup (8 g) chopped fresh cilantro

½ teaspoon salt, plus a pinch

Pinch freshly ground black pepper

2 teaspoons ground cumin

1 teaspoon smoked paprika

1 (1½-pound/680 g) flank or skirt steak

1 tablespoon (15 ml) extra virgin olive oil

12 corn tortillas, store-bought or homemade (page 32), warmed

El Griego Sauce (page 28)

In a medium bowl, combine the cucumber, Kalamata olives, grape tomatoes, lime juice, jalapeño, garlic, and cilantro. Season with a pinch of salt and pepper and set aside.

In a small bowl, mix the cumin, paprika, and ½ teaspoon salt. Season the steak with the mixture on both sides, then brush the olive oil over the steak.

Preheat a grill or heat a large skillet over medium-high heat. Cook the steak for 5 to 7 minutes on the first side, flip, and cook for an additional 5 minutes, or until it reaches your desired doneness.

Transfer the steak to a plate, cover, and let it rest for 15 minutes. Slice the steak thinly against the grain.

To serve, place 2 or 3 steak slices on each tortilla. Top each taco with 1 to 2 tablespoons (15 to 30 g) cucumber salsa and drizzle with some sauce.

KOREAN BEEF TACOS

YIELD: 6 SERVINGS

Wait till you try these tacos—the Asian-flavored beef coupled with the crunchy cabbage and fresh cilantro is a taste explosion waiting to happen with each bite.

¼ cup (60 ml) soy sauce
¼ cup (80 g) honey
¼ cup (60 ml) toasted sesame oil
¼ cup (60 ml) hot water
4 garlic cloves, grated
1 tablespoon (8 g) grated fresh ginger
1 teaspoon freshly ground black pepper
1½ pounds (680 g) skirt or flank steak, very thinly sliced against the grain
12 corn tortillas, store-bought or homemade (page 32), warmed
1 small head purple cabbage, thinly sliced
¼ cup (4 g) fresh cilantro, chopped
1 avocado, pitted, peeled, and sliced
Sriracha-Lime Dressing (page 31)
1 lime, cut into wedges

In a medium bowl, whisk together the soy sauce, honey, sesame oil, hot water, garlic, ginger, and black pepper until the honey dissolves.

Put the steak slices in a large zip-top bag or airtight container and pour in the marinade. Toss around to combine, then seal. Refrigerate for at least 4 hours or overnight for best results.

Heat a large cast-iron skillet over medium-high heat. Remove the steak slices from the marinade with tongs and put them in the skillet (reserve the marinade); you should hear a strong sizzle. Cook for 2 to 3 minutes, until lightly browned on one side, then stir the pieces around and cook for an additional 5 minutes. Reduce the heat to the lowest setting, pour in the marinade, and let it caramelize for about 1 minute. Remove the pan from the heat.

Assemble the tacos by placing several slices of steak on each tortilla. Add some shredded cabbage, cilantro, and avocado slices. Drizzle the dressing over the top and serve with lime wedges on the side.

PHILLY CHEESESTEAK TACOS

YIELD: 6 SERVINGS

"Because everything is better inside a taco" was my answer to my husband's question about why his favorite sandwich was served inside a crispy corn tortilla. Once you try this, you'll love the cheesy goodness in every bite.

1 (1¼-pound/570 g) skirt or flank steak, thinly sliced against the grain
2 tablespoons (30 ml) Worcestershire sauce, divided
½ teaspoon salt, divided
Freshly ground black pepper
8 ounces (224 g) cremini or button mushrooms, sliced
1 medium yellow onion, chopped
1 green bell pepper, seeded and chopped
2 tablespoons (30 ml) vegetable oil, divided
8 slices provolone cheese
12 crunchy corn taco shells, warmed

Put the steak slices in a medium bowl and season with 1 tablespoon (15 ml) of the Worcestershire sauce, ¼ teaspoon of the salt, and a few grinds of black pepper. Stir to coat the beef.

In a large bowl, combine the mushrooms, onion, and bell pepper. Season with the remaining 1 tablespoon (15 ml) Worcestershire, remaining ¼ teaspoon salt, and a few grinds of black pepper. Stir to combine.

In a large cast-iron skillet, heat 1 tablespoon (15 ml) of the oil over medium heat. Add the steak and cook for 6 to 9 minutes, flipping the pieces to cook evenly. Transfer the steak to a plate and cover with another plate to keep warm.

Add the remaining 1 tablespoon (15 ml) oil to the skillet. Add the onion and bell pepper and cook, stirring frequently, for about 5 minutes. Add the mushrooms and cook for an additional 2 minutes, or until tender. Return the steak to the skillet and heat through for 2 minutes. Remove the pan from the heat.

Lay the provolone cheese slices over the beef and vegetable mixture and allow it to melt.

Fill the taco shells with the cheesy skillet mixture and serve.

SLOW COOKER BEEF ROAST TACOS

YIELD: 8 SERVINGS

In this recipe, Taco Tuesday meets beef stew—with a little help from the slow cooker. Leftovers make terrific taco rice bowls later in the week.

1 (2-pound/1 kg) chuck beef roast
2 tablespoons (15 g) Arriba! Seasoning (page 38)
3 garlic cloves, grated
1 medium onion, diced
1 serrano pepper, seeded if desired and finely diced
1 jalapeño, seeded if desired and finely diced
¼ cup (60 ml) water
¼ cup (60 ml) lime juice (about 2 limes)
3 tablespoons (48 g) tomato paste
12 to 16 corn tortillas, store-bought or homemade (page 32), warmed
1½ cups (180 g) shredded cheddar cheese
1 or 2 avocados, pitted, peeled, and sliced
Pico de Gallo (page 23)

Place the roast in the slow cooker and sprinkle the seasoning all over. Add the garlic, onion, and peppers.

In a medium bowl, whisk together the water, lime juice, and tomato paste. Pour the mixture over the beef and vegetables.

Cover and cook on high for 4 to 6 hours or on low for 8 to 10 hours. In the last hour, transfer the roast to a cutting board and shred the beef with two forks. Return the shredded beef to the slow cooker, cover, and continue cooking for the last hour.

To serve, top each tortilla with some of the beef and vegetable mixture. Add shredded cheese, avocado slices, and pico de gallo.

STEAK TACOS WITH CILANTRO CHIMICHURRI

YIELD: 6 TO 8 SERVINGS

I make these regularly during the summer because it's the perfect recipe to fire up the grill. It's magical how this simple green sauce can transform steak into an incredible eating experience. I can't help but dip extra soft corn tortillas into the chimichurri sauce and I know you will, too.

FOR THE MARINADE:

1 orange, juiced

2 limes, juiced

⅓ cup (80 ml) soy sauce

⅓ cup (80 ml) olive oil

1 teaspoon honey

4 garlic cloves, grated

½ cup (8 g) chopped fresh cilantro, stems and leaves

1 (2-pound/1 kg) skirt or flank steak, thinly sliced against the grain

1 large sweet onion, sliced

8 corn tortillas, store-bought or homemade (page 32), warmed

Cilantro Chimichurri (page 27)

Pico de Gallo (page 23)

Easy Pickled Jalapeños and Onions (page 24) (optional)

In a medium bowl, whisk together the marinade ingredients and then transfer the mixture to a large zip-top bag. Add the steak and onion slices. Turn to coat and seal the bag. Refrigerate for at least 4 hours or overnight. Remove the bag from the refrigerator about 30 minutes before you begin cooking.

Heat a large cast-iron skillet over medium-high heat. Cook the steak slices for 6 to 9 minutes, flipping the pieces to cook them evenly. Transfer the steak to a plate, leaving the juices in the skillet.

Add the onion slices to the skillet, reduce the heat to medium, and cook, stirring constantly, until golden and caramelized, 7 to 9 minutes. Add the steak back to the skillet to heat through.

Assemble each taco by layering the steak and grilled onion on a tortilla, then topping with cilantro chimichurri and pico de gallo. Serve with pickled jalapeños and onions on the side, if desired.

LAURA'S TIP: If you prefer grilled steak, don't slice it first. Grill the steak for 5 to 7 minutes per side to reach your desired doneness. Then slice the steak thinly against the grain and assemble the tacos.

SKILLET BEEF TACOS

YIELD: 6 SERVINGS

When it's your favorite night of the week and you forgot to buy taco shells or corn tortillas to pull it off and have no time to make the homemade version, this recipe comes to the rescue. It's not quite a salad, but plan on creating a solid bed of greens.

1 tablespoon (15 ml) vegetable oil
1 large yellow onion, finely chopped
1 pound (455 g) ground beef or turkey
2 bell peppers, any color, seeded and diced
3 tablespoons (22 g) taco seasoning
1½ cups (390 g) Restaurant-Style Salsa (page 20)
3 cups (90 g) baby spinach, coarsely chopped
1½ cups (180 g) shredded cheese, such as Mexican blend, cheddar, or Monterey Jack
½ cup (100 g) sliced black olives
2 romaine lettuce heads, shredded
1 avocado, pitted, peeled, and diced (optional)
Sour cream (optional)
Pico de Gallo (page 23) (optional)
Corn chips (optional)

In a large skillet, heat the oil over medium-high heat. Add the chopped onion and sauté for about 3 minutes, until soft. Add the ground meat, diced bell peppers, and taco seasoning and cook, breaking up the meat as it cooks, for 5 to 7 minutes, until it's cooked through.

Add the salsa and spinach, stir to combine, and heat through. Remove the pan from the heat and sprinkle the shredded cheese and black olives over the meat mixture. Cover and let the cheese melt.

To serve, create a bed of shredded romaine lettuce on each plate. Scoop a serving of the ground meat mixture onto the lettuce and let each diner choose their desired toppings.

FOOD TRUCK TACOS

YIELD: 4 TO 6 SERVINGS

A few years ago, during a trip to Austin, I set my mind to visit as many food trucks as possible. For four days, I ate all the tacos I could find, and my love for handheld, street vendor tacos has never left me.

1 tablespoon (15 ml) vegetable oil

3 pounds (1.5 kg) boneless (country-style) beef ribs, fat trimmed

1 can (4-ounce/115 g) chipotle peppers in adobo sauce

½ cup (120 ml) water

⅓ cup (85 g) barbecue sauce

3 limes, 2 juiced and 1 cut into wedges

2 tablespoons (30 ml) apple cider vinegar

4 garlic cloves, chopped

1 tablespoon (7 g) ground cumin

1 tablespoon (18 g) salt

1 large white onion, finely chopped, divided

8 corn tortillas, store-bought or homemade (page 32), warmed

Pico de Gallo (page 23)

2 avocados, pitted, peeled, and sliced

Sour cream

Chopped fresh cilantro

In a large skillet, heat the oil over medium-high heat. Brown the ribs in batches, 3 to 4 minutes per side. Transfer the browned ribs to the slow cooker.

In a blender, blend the chipotle peppers and adobo sauce, water, barbecue sauce, lime juice, vinegar, garlic, cumin, and salt until smooth. Pour the thick sauce over the ribs. Reserve one-quarter of the chopped onion and put the rest in the slow cooker. Cover and cook on high for 6 hours or on low for 10 hours, or until the meat easily separates between two forks.

In the last couple of hours, use tongs to flip the ribs and distribute the sauce on top of the ribs. When the meat is done, break it up into smaller pieces with two forks.

To assemble the tacos, start with a base of meat on each tortilla, top with some of the reserved chopped raw onion, pico de gallo, sliced avocados, sour cream, and cilantro. Serve with grated cheese and lime wedges on the side if you desire.

LAURA'S TIP: Can't find chipotle peppers in adobo sauce? Substitute ¾ cup (175 ml) enchilada sauce.

MEXICAN SHORT RIB TACOS

YIELD: 6 TO 8 SERVINGS

Tender, braised beef falling off the bone is the star of these Mexican short rib tacos. Cooked low and slow in the oven or the slow cooker with Mexican chiles, these are about as satisfying as it gets. And, to me, they are the epitome of comfort food.

1 tablespoon (15 ml) vegetable oil
6 pounds (3 kg) beef short ribs, fat trimmed
1 can (6-ounce, or 170 g) chipotle peppers in adobo sauce
4 garlic cloves, minced
4 ounces (115 g) tomato paste
¼ cup (60 ml) fresh lime juice
2 tablespoons (30 ml) apple cider vinegar
1 tablespoon (7 g) ground cumin

1 tablespoon (18 g) salt
½ cup (120 ml) beef stock
1 large white onion, finely chopped
2 bay leaves
12 Homemade Tortillas (page 36)
2 avocados, peeled, pitted, and sliced
Pico de Gallo (page 23)
Sour cream

In a large skillet, heat the oil over medium-high heat. Begin to brown the beef ribs in batches until browned on both sides, about 3 to 4 minutes per side. Place them inside a large slow cooker once they've browned.

In a blender, combine the chipotle peppers and adobo sauce, garlic, tomato paste, lime juice, apple cider vinegar, cumin, salt, and beef stock. Blend until the sauce is homogenous. Transfer to the slow cooker and pour over the beef. Add half of the chopped onion, reserving the remaining half for serving, and the bay leaves.

Cover and cook for 6 hours on high or 10 hours on low, until the meat is falling off the bone.

Remove the ribs from the sauce. Remove any excess fat from the ribs; discard the bones and shred the meat. Using a large spoon, skim the fat from the surface of the sauce in the slow cooker. Transfer the meat back to the slow cooker and combine with the sauce.

Serve the beef inside a tortilla and top with the reserved chopped onions, sliced guacamole, pico de gallo, and a dab of sour cream.

ASIAN THAI RIB TACOS

YIELD: 4 TO 6 SERVINGS

Fill your slow cooker and come back to find the meat falling off the bone. Top it off with a savory sauce that is finger-licking good. Three cheers for a low-maintenance recipe with lots of flavor!

1 large rack (about 2 pounds/1 kg) pork baby back ribs
½ cup (120 ml) soy sauce
½ cup (140 g) Sriracha sauce, plus more for serving
½ cup (115 g) packed brown sugar
¼ cup (60 ml) rice wine vinegar
¼ cup (80 g) honey
2 tablespoons (30 ml) toasted sesame oil
2 tablespoons (16 g) grated fresh ginger
3 garlic cloves, grated
2 cups (140 g) shredded purple cabbage
8 corn tortillas, store-bought or homemade (page 32), warmed
¼ cup (20 g) chopped scallion
2 tablespoons (16 g) sesame seeds (optional)

Cut the rack of ribs into 3 or 4 sections and place in the slow cooker.

In a medium bowl, whisk together the soy sauce, Sriracha, brown sugar, vinegar, honey, sesame oil, ginger, and garlic. Pour the sauce over the ribs. Cover and cook on high for 4 to 5 hours, or on low for 8 hours until the meat fully separates from the bones.

Transfer the ribs to a cutting board and shred the meat with two forks; discard the bones. Return the meat to the slow cooker and mix it into the sauce.

To assemble the tacos, place a layer of purple cabbage on each tortilla, top with some shredded rib meat, and sprinkle the scallions and sesame seeds on top. Add additional Sriracha if desired.

BARBECUE PORK TACOS WITH HONEY-MUSTARD SLAW

....

YIELD: 8 TO 10 SERVINGS

The slow cooker never disappoints when it comes to making sure I pull off Taco Tuesday after a busy day. And this recipe combines a flavor combination my family loves (honey mustard) with a practically done-for-you taco.

1⅛ teaspoons salt, divided

⅝ teaspoon freshly ground black pepper, divided

1 teaspoon garlic powder

1 (3-pound/1.5 kg) pork shoulder roast

1½ cups (375 g) barbecue sauce, divided

¾ cup (175 g) mayonnaise

¼ cup (44 g) Dijon mustard

3 tablespoons (60 g) honey

2 tablespoons (30 ml) milk

4 cups (280 g) shredded cabbage

1 cup (110 g) matchstick carrots

½ cup (15 g) chopped fresh cilantro, plus more for serving

12 corn tortillas, store-bought or homemade (page 32), warmed

In a small dish, combine 1 teaspoon of the salt, ½ teaspoon of the pepper, and the garlic powder. Season the pork shoulder roast on all sides and place it in the slow cooker. Add ½ cup (125 g) of the barbecue sauce, cover, and cook on high for 2 hours, then turn it down to low and cook for an additional 6 hours.

While the pork is cooking, make the slaw dressing by whisking together the mayonnaise, Dijon mustard, honey, milk, and remaining ⅛ teaspoon each salt and pepper in a medium bowl. Transfer the dressing to a glass jar, cover, and refrigerate until serving time. (The dressing will keep in the refrigerator for up to 1 week.)

Using two forks, carefully shed the pork inside the slow cooker and discard any large fatty pieces. The pork should pull apart easily; if not, cover and cook on low for an additional 30 minutes to 1 hour. Add the remaining 1 cup barbecue sauce to the slow cooker and toss to combine.

In a large bowl, combine the shredded cabbage, carrots, and chopped cilantro. Drizzle with half of the slaw dressing and toss to combine.

To assemble the tacos, place a layer of slaw on each tortilla, top with shredded pork, drizzle with additional slaw dressing, and sprinkle with cilantro.

CHORIZO AND BUTTERNUT SQUASH TACOS

YIELD: 4 SERVINGS

Originally a quick, midweek skillet recipe in my *Best Grain-Free Family Meals on the Planet* cookbook, this family favorite quickly became a taco night guest.

12 ounces (340 g) fresh chorizo sausage
½ cup (80 g) chopped onion
1 pound (454 g) squash, cut into small cubes
1 teaspoon garlic powder
1 teaspoon ground cumin
2 cups (135 g) finely chopped kale, stems removed
½ lime, juiced
Salt and freshly ground black pepper, to taste
8 corn tortillas, store-bought or homemade (page 32), warmed
¼ cup (35 g) crumbled goat cheese
¼ cup (4 g) chopped fresh cilantro

Remove the chorizo from its casings and cook in a large skillet over medium heat for about 4 minutes. Use a slotted spoon to transfer the chorizo to a plate; leave the drippings in the pan.

Add the onion to the skillet and cook, stirring often, for about 3 minutes, until golden and soft. Add the squash, garlic powder, and cumin and continue to cook for 5 to 7 minutes, until the squash is soft.

Add the kale and cook until wilted, about 2 minutes. Add the cooked chorizo back into the pan and stir to combine. Remove the pan from the heat, add the lime juice, and season with salt and pepper.

To assemble the tacos, place a layer of chorizo and squash mixture on each tortilla, top with some crumbled goat cheese, and sprinkle with cilantro.

LAURA'S TIP: Save time by purchasing frozen cubed squash. Simply thaw and incorporate into the recipe.

QUICK HAWAIIAN PORK TACOS

YIELD: 4 SERVINGS

After an eventful helicopter ride over Hawaii, I could tell that my empty stomach needed food! Inspired by the heavenly tacos I ate that day, this recipe never disappoints—especially since it comes together in less than 30 minutes.

1 tablespoon (15 ml) olive oil
1 (1-pound/455 g) center-cut pork loin, cut into bite-size pieces
1 tablespoon (7 g) Arriba! Seasoning (page 38)
½ cup (83 g) diced fresh pineapple
8 corn tortillas, store-bought or homemade (page 32), warmed
Pineapple Salsa (page 23)
½ cup (65 g) crumbled Cotija cheese

In a large cast-iron skillet, heat the oil over medium-high heat. Add the pork pieces and the seasoning and cook for 7 to 9 minutes, until the pork is cooked through and no longer pink.

Add half of the pineapple to the skillet. Continue cooking for about 2 minutes, until the pineapple has released its juices and become incorporated with the pork into a sauce. Remove the pan from the heat.

To assemble the tacos, place a layer of cooked pork on each tortilla and top with some pineapple salsa and crumbled cheese.

PORK TACOS WITH PINEAPPLE PICO DE GALLO

....

YIELD: 4 TO 6 SERVINGS

This slow cooker pineapple pulled pork recipe can be served in tacos or on its own for a next-day lunch. Quick, easy, and delicious—and always a crowd-pleaser!

1 (2-pound/1 kg) pork tenderloin
1 can (28-ounce/795 g) pineapple chunks, with juice
¼ cup (60 ml) soy sauce
2 tablespoons (20 g) honey
1 can (4-ounce/115 g) tomato paste
1 garlic clove, grated
½ teaspoon freshly ground black pepper
1 cup (240 g) Pico de Gallo (page 23)
8 to 12 corn tortillas, store-bought or homemade (page 32), warmed
4 ounces (115 g) goat cheese, crumbled
Chopped fresh cilantro

Put the pork tenderloin in a slow cooker.

In a medium bowl, whisk together the pineapple juice from the can, soy sauce, honey, tomato paste, grated garlic, and pepper. Pour the sauce over the pork tenderloin. Add all but 1 cup (165 g) of the pineapple chunks to the slow cooker and reserve the remainder for the pico de gallo.

Cover and cook on high for 4 hours or on low for 8 to 10 hours. In the last hour, shred the pork with two forks and toss it in the sauce. Cover and continue cooking for the last hour.

In a medium bowl, combine the pico de gallo and the reserved pineapple chunks.

Assemble the tacos by layering some pulled pork on each tortilla and topping with pineapple pico de gallo, goat cheese, and cilantro.

TEQUILA-LIME PULLED PORK TACOS

YIELD: 6 TO 8 SERVINGS

My friend Sandra made these tacos at a Cinco de Mayo party along with my famous margaritas (page 159). My job was to bring the Pico de Gallo (page 23), lots of freshly made masa (dough) for the Corn Tortillas (page 32), and my Grain-Free Tortillas (page 35). The recipe is one of the simplest ones, and yet, the pork is absolutely delicious.

2 cups (470 ml) chicken broth
1 cup (235 ml) tequila
¼ cup (60 ml) lime juice (about 2 limes)
3 garlic cloves, grated
3 tablespoons (22 g) Arriba! Seasoning (page 38)
1 (3-pound/1½ kg) boneless pork shoulder roast
8 corn tortillas, store-bought or homemade (page 32), warmed
1 jalapeño, seeded and diced
½ red onion, finely chopped
Easy Guacamole (page 19)
4 ounces (115 g) crumbled queso fresco
¼ cup (4 g) chopped fresh cilantro
1 lime, cut into wedges

In a slow cooker, combine the chicken broth, tequila, lime juice, garlic, and seasoning. Add the pork shoulder and turn to cover it with the mixture. Cover and cook on high for 5 to 6 hours, until you can easily separate the pork with a fork. Transfer the pork to a cutting board, shred the meat with two forks, and return it to the slow cooker.

To assemble the tacos, place some pork on each tortilla and top with jalapeño, onion, guacamole, queso fresco, and cilantro. Serve with lime wedges.

CARNITAS LETTUCE CUPS

YIELD: 6 SERVINGS

I love the versatility of carnitas! The crispy texture goes well in so many meals. I serve carnitas in lettuce cups, inside a quesadilla, on top of a salad, over rice—you name it! Make sure you don't skip the pan-frying step, as crisping up the meat on a hot pan is what gives a traditional pork roast the name "carnitas."

2 teaspoons (2 g) dried oregano
1 teaspoon ground cumin
1 teaspoon salt
½ teaspoon freshly ground black pepper
½ teaspoon chili powder
1 tablespoon (15 ml) olive oil
2 pounds (1 kg) boneless pork shoulder roast
1 onion, chopped

4 garlic cloves, minced
1 jalapeño, seeded and minced
1 orange, cut in half
3 tablespoons (45 ml) vegetable oil, divided
1 head Bibb or iceberg lettuce, leaves separated
1½ cups (105 g) shredded cheddar cheese
Pico de Gallo (page 23)
1 lime, cut into wedges

In a small dish, combine the oregano, cumin, salt, pepper, chili powder, and olive oil and rub the mixture all over the pork shoulder roast. Place the pork in the slow cooker. Toss in the onion, garlic, and jalapeño. Squeeze the orange halves into the slow cooker and then add the spent halves. Cover and cook on low for 8 hours or on high 5 hours, until you can easily separate the meat with a fork. Transfer the pork to a cutting board and shred the meat with two forks.

In a large cast-iron skillet, heat half of the vegetable oil. Add half of the carnitas and sauté to crisp the meat around the edges. Transfer the carnitas to a large plate and repeat with the remaining oil and meat.

Layer two lettuce leaves to build each cup and scoop some crispy carnitas into it. Top with shredded cheddar and pico de gallo and serve with lime wedges.

BLACKENED SALMON FAJITA TACOS

YIELD: 4 SERVINGS

If you are the type of person who orders the salmon and vegetable plate at restaurants to stay with your health goals, you are going to love this recipe!

2 limes, 1 juiced and 1 cut into wedges

2 teaspoons Cajun seasoning

1 (1-pound/455 g) salmon fillet, skin removed,
   cut into 4 pieces

3 tablespoons (45 ml) vegetable oil, divided

1 red bell pepper, seeded and sliced

1 onion, sliced

1 cup (150 g) grape tomatoes

1 tablespoon (15 ml) olive oil

¼ teaspoon salt

8 corn tortillas, store-bought or homemade
   (page 32), warmed

1 avocado, pitted, peeled, and sliced

Cilantro-Lime Dressing (page 28)

Preheat the oven to 350°F (180°C) and line a baking sheet with parchment paper.

In a small bowl, combine the juice of 1 lime and the Cajun seasoning. Spread the seasoning mixture on all sides of the salmon pieces.

In a large cast-iron skillet, heat 1 tablespoon (15 ml) of the vegetable oil over medium-high heat. Add the sliced bell pepper and onion and cook, stirring constantly, for 5 to 7 minutes, until crisp-tender. Transfer the vegetables to a plate and tent with aluminum foil to keep warm.

Heat the remaining 2 tablespoons (30 ml) vegetable oil in the skillet. Add the salmon pieces and cook for 3 to 4 minutes, until the bottoms blacken, then flip and cook the other side for 3 to 4 minutes, until blackened. Transfer the salmon to a plate and give it a rough chop into smaller pieces.

While the veggies and salmon cook, put the grape tomatoes on the prepared baking sheet; drizzle with the olive oil and sprinkle with the salt. Roast until the tomatoes start to burst and turn black on a few sides, 5 to 10 minutes.

To assemble the tacos, start with a layer of pepper and onion on each tortilla, top with some salmon, charred tomatoes, and avocado slices, and drizzle with the dressing. Serve with lime wedges.

CHILI-LIME SALMON TACOS

....

YIELD: 4 TO 6 SERVINGS

This is one of those never-fail crowd-pleaser dishes. If you're looking to impress your guests, try these super-tasty tacos—they're perfect for any occasion.

1 (1-pound/455 g) salmon fillet, skin removed, cut into 4 pieces
2 tablespoons (30 ml) olive oil
2 limes, 1 zested and juiced and 1 cut into wedges
1 jalapeño, seeded and minced
½ teaspoon coarse salt
2 cups (350 g) chopped ripe mango
Pico de Gallo (page 23)
1 head butter lettuce, leaves separated
8 to 12 corn tortillas, store-bought or homemade (page 32), warmed
1 avocado, pitted, peeled, and sliced

Preheat the oven to 350°F (180°C) and line a baking sheet with parchment paper.

Place the salmon pieces on the prepared baking sheet. Drizzle with the olive oil and the zest and juice of 1 lime. Sprinkle as much jalapeño over the fish as desired for your preferred heat level, and then sprinkle with the coarse salt as well.

Bake for 10 to 13 minutes, depending on the thickness of the salmon, until it flakes easily with a fork. Transfer the salmon to a plate and give it a rough chop into smaller pieces.

Meanwhile, in a medium bowl, combine the chopped mango and pico de gallo.

To assemble the tacos, place a butter lettuce leaf on each tortilla and top with some salmon, mango pico de gallo, and avocado slices. Serve with additional lime wedges.

PINEAPPLE SHRIMP TACOS

YIELD: 4 TO 6 SERVINGS

No outdoor grill? No problem. These tacos come together in just minutes under the broiler!

1½ pounds (680 g) medium raw shrimp, peeled and deveined
2 cups (330 g) fresh pineapple chunks
3 tablespoons (45 ml) extra virgin olive oil
1 teaspoon chili powder
¾ teaspoon ground cumin
½ teaspoon salt
2 garlic cloves, grated
2 limes, divided
2 cups (140 g) shredded purple cabbage
8 to 12 corn tortillas, store-bought or homemade (page 32), warmed
¼ cup (4 g) chopped fresh cilantro
Easy Guacamole (page 19)

Place an oven rack 5 to 6 inches (12 to 15 cm) from the top and preheat the broiler to high. Coat a rimmed baking sheet with cooking spray.

Thread the shrimp onto wooden skewers, alternating with pineapple chunks. You should be able to get 4 to 6 shrimp on each skewer.

In a medium bowl, combine the olive oil, chili powder, cumin, salt, grated garlic, and the juice of ½ lime. Cut the remaining 1½ limes into wedges and set aside for serving.

Place the skewers on the prepared baking sheet and generously brush the oil and seasoning mixture over the shrimp and pineapple.

Broil for about 2 minutes on each side, carefully flipping the skewers with tongs.

To assemble the tacos, place a generous bed of purple cabbage on each tortilla, top with some cilantro, and add 2 or 3 grilled shrimp pieces and pineapple chunks on top. Serve with the guacamole and lime wedges.

CAJUN SHRIMP TACOS WITH AVOCADO SALSA

YIELD: 6 SERVINGS

My favorite New Orleans flavors take these grilled shrimp to a whole new level. Add some avocado salsa—which, by the way, you'll want to eat on its own—and this taco recipe is one you'll crave often.

1 pound (455 g) jumbo shrimp, peeled and deveined
1 tablespoon (7 g) Cajun seasoning
2 tablespoons (30 ml) olive oil
3 Roma tomatoes, diced
1½ cups (190 g) corn kernels
1 can (15-ounce/428 g) black beans, rinsed and drained
½ red onion, diced
2 avocados, pitted, peeled, and diced
¼ cup (4 g) chopped fresh cilantro, plus more for serving
1 lime, juiced
½ teaspoon salt
12 corn tortillas, store-bought or homemade (page 32), warmed
4 ounces (115 g) feta cheese, crumbled

In a medium bowl, toss the shrimp with the Cajun seasoning.

In a medium skillet, heat the olive oil over medium-high heat. Add the shrimp and cook for 2 minutes, then flip and cook for an additional 1 to 2 minutes, until no longer pink.

In a large bowl, combine the tomatoes, corn, black beans, red onion, avocado, cilantro, lime juice, and salt. Toss to mix well.

Assemble the tacos by placing a scoop of avocado salsa on each tortilla, then add some shrimp and top with crumbled feta and cilantro.

SHEET PAN FAJITA SHRIMP TACOS

YIELD: 4 TO 6 SERVINGS

This is an easy, fast, and delicious dish when you're pressed for time. It all comes together on a single sheet pan and you'll have a delicious meal in 20 minutes from start to finish!

1½ pounds (680 g) large shrimp, peeled and deveined

1 yellow bell pepper, seeded and thinly sliced

1 red bell pepper, seeded and thinly sliced

1 orange bell pepper, seeded and thinly sliced

1 small red onion, thinly sliced

1½ tablespoons (25 ml) extra virgin olive oil

1½ tablespoons (12 g) Arriba! Seasoning (page 38)

½ teaspoon kosher salt

1 lime, cut into wedges

¼ cup (4 g) chopped fresh cilantro

8 to 12 corn tortillas, store-bought or homemade (page 32), warmed

1 avocado, pitted, peeled, and sliced

Preheat the oven to 450°F (230°C) and position an oven rack in the middle of the oven. Generously coat a rimmed baking sheet with cooking spray.

In a large bowl, toss the shrimp, bell peppers, and onion with the olive oil, seasoning, and salt until well coated.

Spread out the shrimp and veggies on the prepared baking sheet and bake for 8 to 10 minutes, until the shrimp are no longer pink.

Squeeze the lime wedges over the shrimp and veggies and sprinkle with the fresh cilantro.

Assemble the tacos by placing a generous amount of the shrimp and veggies on each tortilla and topping with avocado slices.

COCONUT-CRUSTED FISH TACOS

YIELD: 4 SERVINGS

The sweet coconutty fish goes perfectly with the tropical mango salsa, while the creamy avocado and salty Cotija cheese balance it all out.

¾ cup (65 g) unsweetened shredded coconut
½ cup (25 g) panko bread crumbs
2 teaspoons (6 g) Arriba! Seasoning (page 38)
4 (4-ounce/115 g) cod fillets
2 limes, 1 cut into quarters and 1 cut into wedges
Pico de Gallo (page 23)
½ mango, diced
1½ cups (105 g) shredded purple cabbage
8 corn tortillas, store-bought or homemade (page 32), warmed
1 small avocado, pitted, peeled, and sliced
2 tablespoons (16 g) crumbled Cotija cheese
1 jalapeño, seeded and minced

Preheat the oven to 350°F (180°C) and place a wire rack on a rimmed baking sheet.

In a shallow pie dish or plate, combine the coconut, panko bread crumbs, and seasoning.

Pat the cod fillets dry with a paper towel. Squeeze a lime quarter over one fillet, then transfer the fish to the coconut breading and turn to coat on both sides. Place the breaded fish on the wire rack. Repeat with the remaining three limes quarters and cod fillets.

Bake for 15 to 20 minutes, depending on the thickness of the fish, until cooked through. Transfer the fish to a plate and use a fork to break up the fish into smaller pieces.

While the fish cooks, combine the pico de gallo and mango.

To assemble the tacos, make a layer of cabbage on each tortilla, add some fish pieces, and top with mango pico de gallo, avocado slices, Cotija cheese, and jalapeño.

BLACKENED FISH TACOS

YIELD: 4 TO 6 SERVINGS

Blackened fish is a traditional New Orleans flavor and one I couldn't leave out of this cookbook. It transforms the simplest (and least expensive) fish, tilapia, into a sophisticated and delicious meal.

1½ pounds (680 g) tilapia fillets
2 to 3 tablespoons (14 to 22 g) Cajun seasoning
2 cups (140 g) shredded green and purple cabbage
2 limes, 1 juiced and 1 cut into wedges
½ teaspoon kosher salt
12 corn tortillas, store-bought or homemade (page 32), warmed
Cilantro-Lime Dressing (page 28)
Chopped fresh cilantro

Preheat the oven to 425°F (220°C) and place a baking sheet in the oven.

Sprinkle both sides of the tilapia with Cajun seasoning.

Using an oven mitt, remove the hot baking sheet from the oven. Generously coat the hot baking sheet with cooking spray and place the seasoned fish fillets on it. Spray the tops of the fillets and carefully return the baking sheet to the oven. Bake for about 15 minutes, depending on the thickness of the fish, until it's cooked through and flakes easily with a fork.

While the fish is in the oven, toss the cabbage with the juice of 1 lime and the salt in a medium bowl.

To assemble the tacos, place some slaw on each tortilla, top with chunks of blackened fish, and add a generous drizzle of cilantro-lime dressing. Sprinkle with cilantro and serve with lime wedges.

GRILLED FISH TACOS WITH SRIRACHA SOUR CREAM

....

YIELD: 4 SERVINGS

Bring on the heat for your next Taco Tuesday with this recipe. You'll definitely want to make your own dry Sriracha-Like Seasoning (page 38)—it's the spicy fairy dust for food.

2 tablespoons (30 ml) olive oil
2 limes, juiced, divided
1 tablespoon (7 g) + ½ teaspoon (1 g) Sriracha-Like Seasoning (page 38), divided
1 pound (455 g) mahi-mahi fillets
2 tablespoons (30 ml) vegetable oil
½ cup (115 g) sour cream
1½ cups (105 g) shredded cabbage
¼ cup (4 g) chopped fresh cilantro, plus more for serving
1 jalapeño, seeded if desired and sliced (optional)
8 flour tortillas, store-bought or homemade (page 36), warmed
1 cup (120 g) shredded sharp cheddar cheese
Restaurant-Style Salsa (page 20)

In an airtight container or large zip-top bag, combine the olive oil, juice of 1 lime, and 1 tablespoon (7 g) of the seasoning. Add the fish, toss to coat, and seal. Refrigerate for 30 minutes.

In a large skillet, heat the vegetable oil over medium-high heat. Remove the fish from the marinade and place it in the pan. Leave it there for about 5 minutes, until a brown, crispy layer has formed on the bottom. With a spatula, gently flip the fish over and cook for 4 to 5 minutes, until the fish is cooked through. Transfer the fish to a cutting board and coarsely chop it.

In a medium bowl, whisk together the sour cream, remaining juice of 1 lime, and remaining ½ teaspoon (1 g) seasoning. In another bowl, toss together the shredded cabbage, cilantro, and jalapeño, if using.

To assemble the tacos, place a layer of slaw on each tortilla, sprinkle with shredded cheese, top with fish, then add some salsa, Sriracha sour cream, and cilantro.

BAJA FISH TACOS

YIELD: 6 SERVINGS

I still remember the first time I ate one of these crispy, flaky tacos at a small taco joint near Santa Monica Beach when I was in college. It was definitely one of the most memorable and fun moments from the road trip of a lifetime. Invite some friends over and feel free to drink a *cerveza* with these as I did.

24 round crackers (such as Ritz), finely crushed
½ cup (25 g) panko bread crumbs
1 cup (125 g) all-purpose flour
1½ tablespoons (12 g) Arriba! Seasoning (page 38)
1 large egg, lightly beaten
1 cup (235 ml) water
¼ cup (60 ml) lime juice (about 2 limes)
1½ pounds (680 g) mahi-mahi or cod fillets

½ to 1 cup (120 to 235 ml) vegetable oil
1½ cups (105 g) shredded green and purple cabbage
12 corn tortillas, store-bought or homemade (page 32), warmed
1 avocado, pitted, peeled, and sliced
Pico de Gallo (page 23)
Sour cream

In a large bowl, combine the cracker crumbs, panko, flour, seasoning, egg, water, and lime juice into a very thick batter.

Cut the fish into strips about 1 inch (3 cm) thick by 4 inches (10 cm) long. Pat the fish dry between two paper towels so the batter can adhere. Transfer the fish to the batter bowl and use a spatula to mix the fish into the batter to coat all the pieces.

Pour 1 inch (3 cm) of oil into a large cast-iron skillet and heat over medium-high heat until it reaches 375°F (190°C). Remove a few pieces of fish from the bowl, allowing the excess batter to drip back into the bowl, and add them to the skillet. Working in batches, fry the fish until golden, flipping the pieces once to cook the other side. Transfer the fish to a plate lined with paper towels.

Assemble the tacos by placing a thin layer of cabbage on each tortilla, then add some fish pieces and top with avocado slices, pico de gallo, and a generous drizzle of sour cream.

CHAPTER 3

MÁS! REFRESHING BEVERAGES

....

Whether you're hosting a Taco Tuesday fiesta or a weekend gathering with friends, these drinks are staples in nearly all Spanish and Mexican households. *Salud!*

WATERMELON AGUA FRESCA

YIELD: 8 SERVINGS

The first time I tried agua fresca (Spanish for "fresh water") was in Cancún with my friend Jorge. There was a small stand by the beach, and he kindly asked which flavor I'd like. Needless to say, I was smitten at first sip.

2 cups (470 ml) water, divided
¼ cup (80 g) honey
4 cups (600 g) cubed watermelon
4 cups ice

In a microwave-safe bowl, warm ½ cup (120 ml) of the water. Add the honey and stir to dissolve.

Pour the sweetened water into a blender and add the remaining 1½ cups (350 ml) plain water and the watermelon. Blend until smooth.

Strain the watermelon juice through a fine-mesh sieve into a pitcher. Use the back of a spoon to press the watermelon through the sieve. Add the ice to the pitcher and stir.

LIMONADA FRESCA

....

YIELD: 8 TO 10 SERVINGS

In the summer, there's nothing more refreshing than a glass of cold lemonade. I think my kids anticipate the lemonade more than the tacos I'm about to serve sometimes, and that's okay—more tacos for me!

1½ cups (300 g) sugar
8 cups (2 L) water, divided
1½ cups (355 ml) lemon juice, with or without pulp
2 cups ice

In a small saucepan, whisk the sugar and 1 cup (235 ml) of the water over medium heat until the sugar dissolves into the water to create a simple syrup. Remove the pan from the heat and let cool to room temperature. Transfer to an airtight container and refrigerate.

Put the ice in a large pitcher. Add the remaining 7 cups (1.6 L) water, simple syrup, and lemon juice and stir to combine.

HORCHATA MEXICANA

YIELD: 4 SERVINGS

Served over ice and very cold, this rice drink is incredibly refreshing. With hints of cinnamon and a bit of lemon zest, it's a people-pleaser for sure. Want to kick it up a notch? Try the Granizado de Café y Horchata (page 156), where horchata is used to make iced coffee.

1 cup (185 g) uncooked long-grain white rice
3½ cups (825 ml) cold water
1 can (12-ounce/355 ml) evaporated milk
¼ cup (50 g) sugar
1 teaspoon vanilla extract, preferably Mexican
½ teaspoon ground cinnamon
¼ teaspoon grated lemon zest
Ice

Put the rice in a medium bowl and pour in enough water to cover it. Soak the rice overnight. In the morning, strain the rice and discard the water.

Transfer the rice to a blender and add the 3½ cups (825 ml) fresh cold water, evaporated milk, sugar, vanilla, cinnamon, and lemon zest. Blend until the mixture is smooth and the rice is fully incorporated.

Line a strainer with two layers of cheesecloth and place the strainer over a large pitcher. Strain the rice milk through the cheesecloth, wringing out the final drops of liquid through the cheesecloth with your hands. Discard the solids.

Refrigerate the horchata until cold and serve over ice.

HORCHATA ESPAÑOLA

YIELD: 4 SERVINGS

I grew up drinking this classic horchata over ice with my grandmother every summer afternoon while we played cards. It is particularly popular in the Valencia region of Spain, where they grow *chufas* (tiger nuts). While you won't likely find tiger nuts at your regular grocery store, many online retailers sell them. Their earthy, nutty taste makes a nut milk that is unlike any other.

8 ounces (250 g) tiger nuts
3½ cups (825 ml) cold water
¼ cup (50 g) sugar
½ teaspoon ground cinnamon
½ teaspoon grated lemon zest
Ice

Put the tiger nuts in a medium bowl and pour in enough water to cover them. Soak the tiger nuts overnight. In the morning, strain the tiger nuts and discard the water.

Transfer the tiger nuts to a blender and add the 3½ cups (825 ml) fresh cold water, sugar, cinnamon, and lemon zest. Blend until the mixture is smooth and the tiger nuts have fully incorporated.

Line a strainer with two layers of cheesecloth and place the strainer over a large pitcher. Strain the nut milk through the cheesecloth, wringing out the final drops of liquid through the cheesecloth with your hands. Discard the solids.

Refrigerate the horchata until cold and serve over ice.

LAURA'S TIP: I've made both this recipe and the Horchata Mexicana (page 152) without the sugar by replacing it with liquid stevia. You'll need ½ teaspoon liquid stevia to equal ¼ cup (50 g) sugar. The sweetness is easy to adjust with both the sugar and the stevia versions.

GRANIZADO DE CAFÉ Y HORCHATA (COFFEE AND HORCHATA FREEZE)

YIELD: 1 SERVING

My grandmother used to love to take a cup of Horchata Española (page 155) and turn it into a "granizado" by placing it in the freezer for about an hour and a half, until it turned into slush. During the summertime, many *chiringuitos* (beach-side cafés) serve this granizado as a refreshing alternative to iced coffee. Make it once and you'll be hooked.

8 ounces (235 ml) Horchata Española (page 155) or Horchata Mexicana (page 152)
½ to ¾ cup (120 to 175 ml) strong brewed coffee

Fill one cup with the horchata and another cup with the coffee and place both in the freezer for 1 to 1½ hours, just until they turn into slush; poke with a fork to test for doneness. Don't allow them to freeze completely.

In a large cup, gently combine the horchata and coffee. Sip with a straw.

LAURA'S TIP: This recipe can easily be made in larger quantities.

THE PERFECT MARGARITA

YIELD: 1 SERVING

The margaritas I've had in Mexico City are nothing like the sugary drinks served at most bars in the United States. In Mexico, the quality of the tequila sets the tone for this fine drink, and because there is no sugar added to this recipe, the better the tequila, the better the margarita. For years, I tried many different recipes and configurations and at last I discovered this recipe in a *Bon Appétit* magazine in July 2008. I still have the issue on my shelf, reminding me how good this drink really is. I prefer it on the rocks, with no salt, but feel free to rim your glass. *Salud!*

1½ ounces (45 ml) tequila
1½ ounces (45 ml) triple sec or Cointreau
1¼ ounces (40 ml) lime juice
Ice

Combine the tequila, triple sec, and lime juice in a cocktail shaker and shake until the outside becomes frosty. Strain into a glass over ice.

LAURA'S TIP: It's up to you whether to use triple sec or Cointreau; it just depends how boozy you want to get. Triple sec has between 15 and 30 percent alcohol content, depending on the brand, whereas Cointreau is stronger, at 40 percent.

Depending where you live and the time of the year, limes might be very sour, so feel free to add 1 tablespoon (15 ml) agave syrup to the shaker for a slightly sweeter margarita.

SPANISH SANGRIA

YIELD: 4 TO 6 SERVINGS

Few drinks are better than a traditional sangria in Spain, alongside some tapas. Yes, I realize that this is a Mexican taco book, but no party at my house is complete without sangria. You can take the girl out of Spain but can't take Spain out of the girl.

2 tablespoons (25 g) sugar
3 tablespoons (45 ml) water
1 orange, unpeeled, chopped and seeded, plus orange slices for garnish
1 apple, unpeeled, cored and diced
¾ cup (180 ml) orange juice, plus more to taste
⅓ cup (80 ml) brandy (optional)
1 bottle (750 ml) dry red Spanish wine
Ice

In a small saucepan, whisk the sugar and water over medium heat until the sugar dissolves into the water to create a simple syrup. Remove the pan from the heat and let cool to room temperature. Transfer to a large glass pitcher and add the chopped orange. With a muddler or wooden spoon, press down on the orange pieces to release some of their juices. Add the diced apple.

Add the orange juice and brandy, if using, and stir for 30 seconds. Add the red wine and stir to incorporate. Refrigerate for 1 hour.

When ready to serve, add ice to the pitcher and serve in glasses over ice. Garnish each glass with an orange slice.

LAURA'S TIP: The optional brandy adds flavor but also creates a boozier drink; the classic (daytime) sangria omits it.

#TACOTUESDAYBOOK WEEKLY PLAN

Want to celebrate Taco Tuesday with others on social media? Cook a recipe from this book and share it with the hashtag #TacoTuesdayBook on Instagram, Facebook, Twitter, and more.

Don't know where to start? Here is a weekly plan to celebrate Taco Tuesday every week of the year!

WEEK 1: Asian Thai Rib Tacos (page 115)

WEEK 2: Buffalo Chicken Tacos with Homemade Ranch (page 75)

WEEK 3: All-American Beef Tacos (page 95)

WEEK 4: Blackened Zucchini Tacos (page 59)

WEEK 5: Baja Fish Tacos (page 144)

WEEK 6: Black Beans and Queso Breakfast Tacos (page 43)

WEEK 7: Barbecue Pork Tacos with Honey-Mustard Slaw (page 116)

WEEK 8: Quick Carne Asada Tacos (page 96)

WEEK 9: Jamaican Jerk Chicken Tacos (page 76)

WEEK 10: Mexican Short Rib Tacos (page 112)

WEEK 11: Chipotle Beet and Egg Tostadas (page 72)

WEEK 12: Breakfast of Champions Tacos (page 44)

WEEK 13: Grilled Fish Tacos with Sriracha Sour Cream (page 143)

WEEK 14: Carnitas Lettuce Cups (page 127)

WEEK 15: Slow Cooker Chicken Salsa Verde Tacos (page 79)

WEEK 16: Southwestern Tacos (page 71)

WEEK 17: Bacon and Egg Breakfast Tacos (page 55)

WEEK 18: Blackened Fish Tacos (page 140)

WEEK 19: Chorizo and Butternut Squash Tacos (page 119)

WEEK 20: Greek Steak Tacos with Cucumber Salsa (page 99)

WEEK 21: Quick Hawaiian Pork Tacos (page 120)

WEEK 22: Steak and Egg Tacos (page 56)

ACKNOWLEDGMENTS

To my husband, for eating more tacos in nine months than a human should eat in a lifetime. Not that you complained, but I am grateful. Your constant encouragement is always appreciated. Thank you for pushing me through my lows to create incredible things. Together we are better.

To my kids, for deconstructing many of these recipes and telling me how you like to eat them—even if your three ways are different. You guys are awesome.

To Mom, for encouraging me to try new foods. Without you, there would probably be no taco book.

To Yanni, because we taco-bout it a lot. Thanks for always being a great zero-judgment sounding board.

To my friend, Alison Bickel, for teaching me so much about photography and fresh food over the years. While we each have three kids, this fourth book feels like another. We've done well, my friend.

To my editor, Amanda, and the publishing team at Quarto for being as excited about the Taco Tuesday idea as I am.

To all the taco-holics out there, for pushing me to give you the most variety possible in this book while keeping things simple. Enjoy!

To our Creator: With you, all things are possible.

ABOUT THE AUTHOR

Laura Fuentes is the founder of MOMables.com, where she helps thousands of parents make fresh foods for their families with weekly meal plans.

Laura is the author of three other cookbooks: *The Best Homemade Kids' Lunches on the Planet*, *The Best Homemade Kids' Snacks on the Planet*, and *The Best Grain-Free Family Meals on the Planet*. She's a regular contributor to numerous print magazines, *Today*, the Huffington Post, and other online publications.

Laura's passion for teaching parents how to make fresh meals expands beyond print into video. She's competed on the Food Network (and won!), appeared on *Today* and *Good Morning America*, and regularly shares cooking videos in her MOMables YouTube channel.

In her personal blog, LauraFuentes.com, Laura writes about living a fresh and healthy lifestyle as a family, homeschooling her kids, and travel. Above all, her most important job is caring for her family.

INDEX